INDIAN TRIBES of WASHINGTON, OREGON & IDAHO

Originally published by the Smithsonian Institution, Washington, D. C., to which source I give my thanks.

Printing from the workshop of Glen Adams, which is located in the quiet country village of Fairfield, Spokane County, Wn.

INDIAN TRIBES OF WASHINGTON, OREGON & IDAHO

JOHN REED SWANTON

YE GALLEON PRESS
FAIRFIELD, WASHINGTON

Library of Congress Cataloging in Publication Data

Swanton, John Reed, 1873-1958
Indian Tribes of Washington, Oregon and Idaho.

Reprint of the 1952 edition published by the Govt. Print. Off., Washington, which was issued as Bulletin 145 of the Bureau of American Ethnology, Smithsonian Institution.

1. Indians of North America—Washington (State). 2. Indians of North America—Oregon. 3. Indians of North America—Idaho. I. Title. II Series: United States Bureau of American Ethnology. Bulletin; 145.
[E78.W3S9 1978] 979'.004'97 79-1010
ISBN 0-87770-218-7 paper binding
ISBN 0-87770-218-5 hard case

INDIAN CRADLE, WASHINGTON TERRITORY

SMLuke

INDIAN TRIBES OF WASHINGTON, OREGON & IDAHO

IDAHO

Bannock. From their own name Bana'kwŭt. Also called:

Diggers, by many writers.
Ogoize, by the Kalispel.
Panai'ti, form of name given by Hoffman (1886).
Pun-nush, by the Shoshoni.
Robber Indians, by Ross (1855).
Ush-ke-we-ah, by the Crow Indians.

Connections.—The Bannock belonged to the Shoshonean branch of the Uto-Aztecan linguistic stock, being a detached branch of the Northern Paiute.

Location.—In historic times their main center was in southeastern Idaho, ranging into western Wyoming, between latitude 42° and 45° North and from longitude 113° West eastward to the main chain of the Rocky Mountains. At times they spread well down Snake River, and some were scattered as far north as Salmon River and even into southern Montana. (See also Colorado, Oregon, and Utah.)

Subdivisions

A few local group names have been preserved, such as the Kutsshundika or Buffalo-eaters, Penointikara or Honey-eaters, and Shohopanaiti or Cottonwood Bannock, but these are not well defined.

History.—Bridger met the Bannock Indians in the country above indicated as early as 1829, but contacts between them and the Whites became much more intimate with the establishment of Fort Hall in 1834. In 1869 Fort Hall Reservation was set aside for them and the Shoshoni, but they were in the habit of wandering widely and it was a long time before they were gathered into it. They claimed the territory in southwestern Montana in which are situated Virginia City and Bozeman, and it is probable that they were driven across the mountains into the Salmon River Valley at a comparatively recent period. Before 1853 they were decimated by the smallpox and were finally gathered under the Lemhi and Fort Hall agencies. Loss of their lands, failure of the herds of buffalo, and lack of prompt relief on the part of the Government occasioned an uprising of the tribe in 1878, which was suppressed by General O. O. Howard.

Population.—Bridger, in 1829, stated that the Bannock had 1,200 lodges, or a population of about 8,000, but he evidently included the neighboring Shoshoni. Mooney (1928) estimated that in 1845 there were about 1,000, but Forney, in 1858 (p. 213) gave only 400 to 500. In 1870 Jones estimated 600 and Mann 800 "Northern Bannocks." In 1901 they numbered 513 but were so intermixed with Shoshoni that the figure is uncertain. The census of 1910 reported 413, all but 50 of whom were in Idaho, and the census of 1930 gave 415, including 313 in Idaho. In 1937, 342 were reported.

Connections in which they have become noted.—The only prominence attained by the Bannock was for a brief period during the Bannock War. The name is perpetuated by a river, a range of mountains, and a county. There is also a place named Bannock in Belmont County, Ohio, and another in Butler County, Ky., but these are probably not connected with the tribe.

Kalispel. From a native term said to mean "Camas"; they were given the name Pend d'Oreilles, because when they were first met by Europeans nearly all of them wore large shell earrings. Also called:

Ak-min'-e-shu'-me, by the Crow and meaning "the tribe that uses canoes".
Camas People, a translation of Kalispel.
Earring People, an English translation of Pend d'Oreilles.
Hanging Ears, English translation of Pend d'Oreilles.
Ni-he-ta-te-tup'i-o, Siksika name.
Papshpûn'lĕma, Yakima name, signifying "people of the great fir trees."

Connections.—The Kalispel belonged to the interior division of the great Salishan family.

Location.—On Pend Oreille River and Lake, Priest Lake, and the lower course of Clark's Fork. They were said to have extended eastward to Thompson Lake and Horse Plains and to have hunted over some of the Salmon River country, Canada, and were formerly said to have extended to Flathead Lake and Missoula. (See also Montana and Washington.)

Subdivisions

(1) Upper Kalispel or Upper Pend d'Oreilles (in Montana from Flathead Lake and Flathead River to about Thompson Falls on Clark Fork of the Pend Oreille River, including the Little Bitterroot, southward about to Missoula and northward to the International Boundary), with bands at Flathead Lake, near Kalispel, at or near Dayton, near Polson at the foot of the lake, and possibly one at Columbia Falls; some wintered on the Bitterroot and a large band at St. Ignatius.

(2) Lower Kalispel or Lower Pend d'Oreilles or Kalispel proper (from Thompson Falls down Clark Fork, Pend Oreille Lake, Priest Lake, and Pend Oreille River nearly to the International Boundary and hunting territories along Salmon River, British Columbia).

(3) The Chewelah (in the country west of the Calispell or Chewelah Mountains in the upper part of the Colville Valley).

The Lower Kalispel also included several minor bands, the Chewelah apparently two. The Chewelah subdivision spoke a slightly different dialect and was sometimes regarded as an independent tribe.

History.—The Kalispel were visited by Lewis and Clark in 1805, and in 1809 a post was established on Pend Oreille Lake by the Northwest Company and another on Clark Fork the same year called Salish House. Emissaries of the American Fur Company reached them later, and in 1844 they were missionized by the Roman Catholic Church. July 16, 1855, the Upper Kalispel, Kutenai, and Salish surrendered all of their lands except an area about Flathead Lake which became the Jocko Reservation. The greater part of the Kalispel settled here, but part of the Lower Kalispel were gathered on Colville Reservation with the Okanagon, Colville, and a number of other tribes.

Population.—Mooney (1928) estimated that the Kalispel numbered 1,200 in 1780, but Teit (1930) considered that the prehistoric population must have been between 5,000 and 6,500, an estimate which would seem to be excessive. In 1805 Lewis and Clark estimated that there were 30 lodges of these people and a population of 1,600. In 1905 there were 640 Upper and 197 Lower Pend d'Oreilles under the Flathead Agency (Jocko Reservation) and 98 under the Colville Agency. The census of 1910 reported 386 from Montana, 157 from Washington, 15 from Idaho, and 6 from three other States. They were not separately enumerated in 1930, but the United States Office of Indian Affairs reported 97 in 1937.

Connections in which they have become noted.—The name Kalispel is preserved in that of the banking city of Kalispell, county seat of Flathead County, Mont., by Calispell Lake, and by the Calispell Mountains. The name Pend d'Oreilles is preserved in Pend Oreille Lake in northern Idaho and in Pend Oreille River in Montana, Idaho, and Washington.

Kutenai. This tribe occupied the extreme northern part of Idaho. (See Montana.)

Nez Percé. A French appellation signifying "pierced noses." Also called:

Â'dal-k'ato'igo, Kiowa name, signifying "people with hair cut across the forehead."
Anípörspi, Calapooya name.
A-pa-o-pa, Atsina name (Long, 1823).

A-pū-pe', Crow name, signifying "to paddle," "paddles."
Blue Muds, name applied by traders.
Chopunnish, Lewis and Clark.
Green Wood Indians, Henry-Thompson Journal.
I'-na-cpĕ, Quapaw name.
Kamŭ'inu, own name.
Ko-mun'-i-tup'-i-o, Siksika name.
Mikadeshitchísi, Kiowa Apache name.
Nimipu, own name, signifying "the people."
Pa ka'-san-tse, Osage name, signifying "plaited hair over the forehead."
Pe ga'-zan-de, Kansa name.
Pierced Noses, English translation of name.
Po'-ge-ħdo-ke, Dakota name.
Sa-áptin, Okanagon name.
Shi'wanĭsh, Tenino name for this tribe and the Cayuse, signifying "strangers from up the river."
Tchaχsúkush, Caddo name.
Thoig'a-rik-kah, Shoshoni name, signifying "louse eaters(?)."
Tsuhárukats, Pawnee name.
Tsútpĕli, own name.

Connections.—The Nez Percé Indians were the best known tribe of the Shahaptian division of the Shapwailutan linguistic stock, to which they gave the name commonly applied to them by Salish tribes.

Location.—The Nez Percé occupied a large part of central Idaho, and sections of southeastern Washington and northeastern Oregon. (See also Montana and Oklahoma.)

Subdivisions

The following bands are given by Spinden (1908):

Alpowē'ma, on Alpaha (Alpowa) Creek.
Atskaaiwawixpu, at the mouth of the northern fork of Clearwater River.
Esnime, Slate Creek Band, the Upper Salmon River Indians.
Hasotino, at Hasutin, opposite Asotin City, Wash.
Hatwēme, on Hatweh Creek.
Heswéiwewipu, at the month of Asotin Creek.
Hĭnsepu, at Hansens Ferry on the Grande Ronde.
Imnáma, on Imnaha River.
Inantoĭnu, at the mouth of Joseph Creek.
Isăwisnemepu, near Zindels, on the Grande Ronde.
Iwatōĭnu, at Kendrick on Potlatch Creek.
Kamiaxpu, at Kamiah, at the mouth of Lawyer's Creek; this band also called Uyame.
Lamtáma, on Salmon River.
Lapwēme, on Lapwai and Sweetwater Creeks.
Makapu, on Cottonwood or Maka Creek.
Painīma, near Peck, on Clearwater River.
Pipū'ĭnĭmu, on Big Cañon Creek.
Saiksaikinpu, on the upper portion of the Southern Fork of Clearwater River.
Sakánma, between the mouth of Salmon River and the mouth of Grande Ronde.
Sálwēpu, on the Middle Fork of Clearwater River, about 5 miles above Kooskia, Idaho.

Saxsano, about 4 miles above Asotin City, Wash., on the east side of Snake River.
Simīnekempu, at Lewiston, Idaho.
Taksehepu, at Agatha on Clearwater River.
Tamanmu, at the mouth of Salmon River.
Tewepu, at the mouth of Oro Fino Creek.
Toiknimapu, above Joseph Creek on the north side of the Grande Ronde.
Tsokolaikiinma, between Lewiston and Alpowa Creek.
Tukē'lĭklīkespu, at Big Eddy.
Tukpăme, on the lower portion of the South Fork of Clearwater River.
Tunèhepu, at Juliaetta on Potlatch Creek.
Walwáma, in Willowa Valley.
Wewī'me, at the mouth of the Grande Ronde.
Witkispu, about 3 miles below Alpowa Creek, on the east side of Snake River.
Yaktō'ĭnu, at the mouth of Potlatch Creek.
Yatóīnu, on Pine Creek.

The Nuksiwepu, Sahatpu, Wawawipu, Almotipu, Pinewewewixpu, Tokalatoinu, and other bands extended about 80 miles down Snake River from Lewiston.

History.—In 1805 Lewis and Clark passed through the territory of the Nez Percé Indians. The first friction between this tribe and the Whites followed upon the discovery of gold in the West and the consequent influx of miners and settlers. By treaties concluded in 1855 and 1863 they ceded all of their lands to the United States Government with the exception of one large reservation. The occupants of Wallowa Valley refused to agree to the final cessions, and the Nez Percé war of 1877 resulted, distinguished by the masterly retreat of Chief Joseph toward the Canadian line, which was almost attained by him before he was overtaken. Joseph and his followers to the number of 450 were sent to Oklahoma, but they lost so heavily from disease that in 1885 they were removed to the Colville Reservation, Wash., where a few still live.

Population.—Mooney (1928) estimates a population of 4,000 Nez Percé in 1780. In 1805 Lewis and Clark computed the total number at 6,000, if we deduct the estimated population of the two tribes later reckoned as distinct. Wilkes (1849) gives 3,000 and Gibbs (1877) estimates more than 1,700 in 1853. In 1885 the official figure was 1,437. In 1906 there were 1,534 on Lapwai Reservation and 83 on Colville Reservation, Wash. The census of 1910 reported 1,259, of whom 1,035 were in Idaho. The Report of The United States Indian Office for 1923 gave 1,415 and the report for 1937, 1,426. In 1930 the Shahaptian division of the Shapwailutan stock numbered 4,119.

Connections in which they have become noted.—The Nez Percé have claims to remembrance, (1) as the largest and most powerful tribe of the Shapwailutan stock, (2) as having given a name applied to them to the principal division of the formerly independent Shahaptian family. From this tribe Nez Perce County, Idaho, and the post village of Nezperce in Lewis County derive their names.

Paiute, Northern. Indians of this group entered the southwestern part of Idaho at times. (See Nevada.)

Palouse. This tribe extended up the Palouse River into Idaho. (See Washington.)

Salish, or **Flathead.** The present State of Idaho was visited to some extent by Indians of this tribe. (See Montana.)

Shoshoni, Northern. Significance of the word Shoshoni is unknown. Also called:

Aliatan, a name taken originally from that of the Ute and subsequently applied to many Shoshoni tribes, including the Shoshoni proper.
Bik-ta'-she, Crow name, signifying "grass lodges."
E-wu-h'a'-wu-si, Arapaho name, signifying "people that use grass or bark for their houses or huts."
Gens du Serpent, by the French.
Ginebigônini, Chippewa name, signifying "snake men."
Kinebikowininiwak, Algonkin name, signifying "serpents."
Ma-buc-sho-roch-pan-ga, Hidatsa name.
Miká-atí, Hidatsa name, signifying "grass lodges."
Mi'kyashč, Crow name, signifying "grass lodges."
Pezhi'-wokeyotila, Teton Dakota name, signifying "grass-thatch dwellers."
Pi-ci'-kse-ni-tup'i-o, Siksika name.
Sin-te'-hda wi-ca-sa, Yankton Dakota name, signifying "rattlesnake Indians."
Sisízhanín, Atsina name signifying "rattlesnake men."
Snake Indians, common English name.
Snóă, Okanagon name.
Wákidohka-numak, Mandan name, signifying "snake man."
Wĕs'ănikaciⁿga, Omaha and Ponca name, signifying "snake people."
Zuzéca wićása, Teton Dakota name, signifying "snake people."

Connections.—The Northern Shoshoni belonged to the Shoshoni-Comanche dialectic group of the Shoshonean division of the Uto-Aztecan linguistic family.

Location.—The Northern Shoshoni occupied eastern Idaho, except the territory held by the Bannock; western Wyoming; and northeastern Utah.

Subdivisions

Their only subdivisions were a number of bands headed by popular chiefs, the make up of which was constantly shifting.

Villages

Lemhi and Central Idaho:
Bohodai, near the junction of Middle Fork with the Salmon, and an unnamed site on upper Salmon River where a few families from Sohodai sometimes wintered.
Guembeduka, about 7 miles north of the town of Salmon.
Padai, scattered along Lemhi River about Salmon.

Pagadut, on Red Rock Creek, about Lima, Mont.; possibly a few families lived near Dillon, Mont.
Pasasigwana, at a warm spring in the mountains north of Clayton.
Pasimadai, on Upper Salmon River.
Sohodai, on the upper Middle Fork of Salmon River, near Three Rivers.

Fort Hall Shoshoni:
No band names given.

Bannock Creek (Kamdüka) Shoshoni (Pocatello's Band):
Biagamugep, the principal village, near Kelton.

Cache Valley (Pangwiduka) Kwagunogwai:
Along the Logan River above its junction with the Little Bear River.

Salt Lake Valley:
There are said to have been bands in the Ogden, Weber, and Salt Lake Valleys, but their names have not been preserved; they are sometimes called Ute, but Steward is certain that they were affiliated with the Shoshoni.

History.—At one time the Northern Shoshoni extended farther eastward into the Plains but there is no reason to suppose that they did not at the same time retain the mountain territories later held by them. They were affected only indirectly by the Spanish settlements to the south and southwest. In 1805 they were met by Lewis and Clark who were guided by a famous woman of their nation, Sacagawea, and from that time on contact with the Americans became fairly common. The Northern Shoshoni, particularly those under the famous chief Washakie, were unusually friendly to the Whites. They were finally gathered upon the Lemhi and Fort Fall Reservations in Idaho and the Wind River Reservation in Wyoming. By the Treaty of Fort Bridger, July 3, 1868, the eastern bands of the Shoshoni and Bannock ceded all rights to their territories in Wyoming and Idaho except the Wind River Reservation in the former state for the Shoshoni and a reservation to be set apart for the Bannock whenever they desired it. On July 30, 1869, Fort Hall Reservation was set aside for the Bannock but subsequently occupied in part by the Shoshoni. February 12, 1875, the Lemhi Reservation was established for these two tribes and the Sheepeater band of Western Shoshoni.

Population.—Mooney (1928) estimated 4,500 in the year 1845, including the Western Shoshoni. The United States Census of 1910 gave 3,840 "Shoshoni," of which number about 2,000 appear to have belonged to this division. The Report of the Office for Indian Affairs of 1917 indicated about 2,200. The census of 1930 reported 3,994 for the Northern and Western Shoshoni combined, but in 1937 the United States Office of Indian Affairs reported 3,650 Northern Shoshoni alone.

Connections in which they have become noted.—The Northern Shoshoni are the most prominent and strongest tribe of the upper plateau. They were also distinguished by the fact that their name was employed by Gallatin (1936) and later adopted by Powell (1891) for application to a linguistic stock, a stock now considered a branch of a much larger group, the Uto-Aztecan. The Shoshoni came into prominence in the last century (1) because Sacagawea or Bird Woman, the famous guide and interpreter of Lewis and Clark in their expedition to the Pacific, was a member of this tribe; and (2) because of the ability of chief Washakie and his constant friendship for the Whites. The name Shoshone has been applied to rivers and mountains in Wyoming and Nevada; to a lake in Yellowstone National Park; to the Shoshone Falls of Snake River; to a county in Idaho; and to places in Inyo County, Calif.; Lincoln County, Idaho; White Pine County, Nev.; and Fremont County, Wyo.

Shoshoni, Western. Significance of the word Shoshoni is unknown.

Connections.—The same as for the Northern Shoshoni.

Location.—Central and western Idaho, northwestern Utah, central and northeastern Nevada, and a small territory in California north of and about Death and Panamint Valleys.

Subdivisions

The names of a great many local groups have been recorded, usually signifying that they were "eaters" of certain kinds of food, but most of these seem to have belonged to territories rather than people, the "eaters" in each being subject to change. A few of these have, however, acquired special interest and some measure of permanence as, for instance, the Tukuarika, Tukuadüka, or Sheep Eaters, extending from the Yellowstone National Park to the middle course of Salmon River; the Gosiute of northern Utah and eastern Nevada and the Panamint or Koso, the Californian representatives of the division.

Villages

Steward (1938) gives the following villages under the several natural areas occupied by these Indians:

Lida and vicinity:
- Clayton Valley.
- Kamuva, or Wipa, several miles east of Goldfield.
- Montezuma.
- Old Camp, on the north side of Gold Mountain.
- Pauwaha' (Lida).
- Tumbasai'uwi, at Stonewall Mountain.

Eastern California:
- Saline Valley:
  - Isha'mba (Waucoba Spring).
  - Ko (Saline Valley).
  - Navadu, at the Springs in Cottonwood Canyon which runs west from Death Valley.
  - Tuhu, at Goldbelt Spring.
- Little Lake and Koso Mountains:
  - Mua'ta (Coso Hot Springs).
  - Pagunda (Little Lake).
  - Pakwa'si (at Alancha).
  - Uyuwu'mba, about 5 miles south of Darwin.

Panamint Valley:
No villages given.
Northern Death Valley:
Mahunu (springs in Grapevine Canyon and probably Grapevine Springs).
Ohyu, at Surveyor's Well.
Panuga (Mesquite Springs).
Central and Southern Death Valley:
Tumbica, at the several springs at Furnace Creek.
Village (perhaps) some 15 miles south of Furnace Creek.
Beatty and Belted Mountains (camps):[7]
Howell Ranch, near Springdale.
Hunusu, at Burn's Ranch.
Indian Camp, at the head of Oasis Valley.
Mutsi, in the vicinity of the water holes marked merely "Tanks" on the U. S. Geol. Surv. map.
Sivahwa, a few miles north of the last.
Tunava, at Whiterock Springs.
Takanawa, at Hick's Hot Springs.
Sakaiñaga, at the mouth of Beatty Wash on the Amagrosa River.
Panavadu, somewhere near the last.
Wuniakuda, 2 or 3 miles east of the Ammonia Tanks.
Wiva, at Oaksprings.
Kuikun (Captain Jack Spring).
Tupipa, at Tippipah Springs.
Pokopa, at Topopah Spring.
Pagambuhan (Cane Spring).
Ione Valley, Reese River, and Smith Creek Valley:
Reese River Valley (camps):[7]
Wiyunutuahunupi, at the first creek south of Austin.
Angasikigada, 1 mile from the last.
Tutumbihunupi, 1½ miles from the last.
Ohaogwaihunupi, 1 mile from the last.
Bambishpahunupi, about 2 miles from last.
Songwatumbihun, about 1½ miles from the last.
Gunuvijep, about 1½ miles from the last.
Biahunupi, at Big Creek, west of Kingston.
Mezaguahunupi, 2 miles from the last.
Oapihunupi, 2 miles from the last.
Tudupihunupi, 1½ miles from the last.
Yudigivoihunupi, 2 miles from the last.
Aihyuhunupi, about 2 miles from the last.
Navahodava, 3 miles from the last.
Guvadakuahunupi, 2 miles from the last or about halfway between Austin and Bell's Ranch.
Baiambasahunupi, about 1 mile from the last.
Kwinahunupi, 2 miles from the last.
Tosakuahunupi, 3 miles from the last.
Asunguahunupi, 1 mile from the last.
Wakaihunupi, 1 mile from the last.
Boyuwihunupi, 3 miles from the last.
Yumbahunupi, 3 miles from the last.
Onihunupi, about 2½ miles from the last.

[7] Camps given in order of location; names not alphabetized.

Adumbihunupi, about 2½ miles from the last.
Bukwiyohunupi, about 4 miles from the last and a little south of Bell's Ranch

Reese River Valley (winter sites): [8]

Sunungoi, about 10 miles northwest of Austin and slightly north of Mount Airy.
Sova, a spring near the summit of Mount Airy.
Tuosava, 2 or 3 miles south of the last.
Yutomba, 1 mile from the last.
Evimba, 3 or 4 miles from the last.
Dumboi, 2 or 3 miles from the last.
Hukumba, about 2 miles from the last.
Kosiva, 3 miles from the last.
Wupayagahunupi, 3 miles from the last.
Dawishiwuhunupi, 2 miles from the last.
Kunuvidumbihunupi, about 1½ miles from the last.
Pazuyohoi, 4 miles from the last.
Wangodusikihunupi, 2 miles from the last.
Ava, 2 miles from the last.
Bohoba, a spring 3 miles from the last.
Dongwishava, slightly south of Ione, west of the Bell Ranch.
There is also a camp southwest of Berlin Peak at a spring called Wanzi awa.

Great Smoky Valley and Monitor Valley:

No villages given.

Kawich Mountains (winter camps):

Breen Creek.
Hot Creek, about 10 miles north of Tybo.
Hot Springs, to the south, had several winter encampments.
Hugwapagwa (Longstreet Canyon or Horse Canyon).
Kunugiba (Tybo Creek).
Reveille Mill.
Tuava (Rose Spring).

Little Smoky Valley and vicinity:

Little Smoky Valley:

Dzishava (Moore Station).
Indian Creek (Bagumbush?), 6–7 miles north of Kwadumba.
Kwadumba (Snowball), 8 miles north of Sapava.
Kwatsugu (Fish Creek).
Sapava (Hick's Station), 12 miles north of Morey.
Tutoya, at a spring 4 or 5 miles south of Morey, on the west side of the valley.

Fish Springs Valley:

Butler's Place, about 20 miles north of Wongodoya.
Udulfa (Hot Creek).
Wongodoya, at a spring in the hills west of Fish Springs.

Railroad Valley (camps in north end of valley):

Akamba, or probably also Watoya, at a spring west of Mount Hamilton.
Bambasa, on the west side of Mount Hamilton.
Bauduin (Warm Spring).
Bawazivi (Currant Creek).
Biadoyava, at Blue Eagle Springs.
Nyala, native name unknown.
Suhuva (Duckwater).
Wongodupijugo, southeast of Green Spring.

---

[8] Winter sites given in order of location; names not alphabetized.

Steptoe Valley:
"There were . . . villages at Ely, on Duck Creek, about 8 miles northwest of McGill, and at Warm Spring, Schellbourne, Egan Canyon, and Cherry Creek."
Spring, Snake, and Antelope Valleys:
Spring Valley:
Aidumba, at a spring west of Aurun.
Basamba, slightly up the hill west of Sogowosugu.
Basiamba, in vicinity of Oceola.
Basawinuba, either 3 or 4 miles northwest of Aurun.
Basawinuba (Mud Springs), about 7 miles south of Aurun.
Basonip, about 7 miles (?) south of Cleveland Ranch.
Bauumba, near Shoshone.
Biabauwundu, at Cleveland Ranch.
Haiva, about 6 miles north of Cleveland or two canyons south of Wongovitwuninogwap.
Sogowosugu, at Aurun.
Supuva, at Anderson's Ranch.
Taiwudu, on west slope of Snake Mountains.
Toziup, on west slope of Mount Moriah.
Tuhuva, between Yellen's and Cleveland Ranches.
Tupa, about 7 miles north of Anderson's Ranch.
Wongovitwuninogwap, on Valley Creek, about 10 miles north of Cleveland
Antelope Valley:
Bohoba, at Mike Springs south of the villages in Antelope Valley.
Hugapa, at Chinn Creek.
Kwadumba, at a spring about 3 miles south of Tippetts.
Suhuva, at a spring near Kwadumba.
Toiva, at a spring at north end of valley.
Wadoya, at a spring 15 miles north of Toiva.
Snake Valley:
Bauwunoida, at the present Baker.
Biaba, at Big Spring.
Tosakowaip, at Silver Creek.
Tunkahniva, near a cave near Lehman Cave in the canyon west of Baker.
Cave Valley, south of Steptoe Valley:
Daint.
Gosiute Shoshoni:
A cave on the north end of the Skull Valley Mountains a short distance from the present highway.
Haiyashawiyep, near present town called Iosepa.
Iowiba, in mountains just east of Skull Valley Reservation.
Ongwove, a few miles south of Orr's Ranch.
Suhudaosa, at the present Orr's Ranch (?).
Tiava, on present reservation.
Tozava, at a spring on west side of Lakeside Range.
Tutiwunupa, on west slope of the Cedar Mountains, just east of Clive.
Utcipa, south of Tutiwunupa on west slope of Cedar Mountains.
Wanapo'ogwaipi, at Indian Springs, south of Ongwove.
Pine Creek and Diamond Valley:
Bauwiyoi, a group of at least 6 encampments at the foot of the Roberts Mountains.

Todzagadu, on the west side of the Sulphur Spring Mountains.
Tupagadu, west of the Alkali flat in Diamond Valley.

Ruby Valley and Vicinity:
A settlement on south side of Spruce Mountains.
A village on the east slope of the Pequop Mountains.
Baguwa, in the flats near Overland.
Butte Valley, at north end on a canyon called Natsumbagwic.
Medicine Spring, on the west slope of the Cedar Mountains, east of Franklin Lake.
Suhuwia, on the headwaters of Franklin River.
Toyagadzu (Clover Valley).
Waihamuta, on the creek against the hills, west of the Neff Ranch.
Wongogadu, on north side of Spruce Mountains.
Yuogumba or Sihuba (Long Valley).

Humboldt River (districts):
A village in a valley a little south of Elko.
A village somewhere on upper Huntington Creek.
Banadia, scattered along both sides of Lamoille Creek.
Badukoi, village about 3 miles below Carlin.
Elko, preferred site for village being at the mouth of the South Fork.
Independence Valley, in the valley of what is called Magpie or Maggie Creek.
Kinome, 5 miles north of Huntington.
Palisade, people lived near here along Humboldt River.
Sahoogep, at Lee.
The valley of North Fork.
Toyagadzu, at Wells.
Tukwampandai, at Deeth.

Battle Mountain and Vicinity:
There was a concentration of population between Battle Mountain and Iron Point.

Snake River (three villages between Hagerman and Bruneau):
Ototumb, near Bliss.
Pazintumb, about 8 miles below Hagerman.
Saihunupi, about 4 miles below Hagerman.

Boise River and Vicinity:
No village names recorded.

Grouse Creek:
Kuiva, on Raft River, probably near Lynn and Yost.
O'o or Podongoe, a little southwest of Lucin.
Paduyavavadizop (Dove (?) Creek).
Tusaid or Angapuni (Grouse Creek).

Promontory Point (Hukundu''ka):
Nagwituwep, on Blue Creek, north of the old railroad.
Nanavadzi, near Little Mountain, east of Promontory Point.
Sudotsa, scattered along valley of Bear River from near Bear River City to Deweyville.
Tongishavo, on the west side of Promontory Point near Mount Tarpey.

The following names, derived from various sources, may be appended:

Kaidatoiabie (with 6 subbands), in northeastern Nevada.
Nahaego, in Reese River Valley, and about Austin, Nev.
Pagantso (with 3 subbands), in Ruby Valley, Nev.

Sunananahogwa, on Reese River, Nev.
Temoksee, in Reese River Valley, Nev.
Toquimas, in lower Reese River Valley, Nev.

History.—The history of the Western Shoshoni was practically identical with that of the Northern Shoshoni and Northern Paiute, except that their territory was somewhat more remote from the paths followed by American explorers in the north and Spaniards in the south. In 1825 Jedidiah Smith made several journeys across Nevada and may have been preceded by Old Greenwood. In 1847 the Mormons settled Nevada and came in contact with some of the eastern representatives of this Shoshonean division. Narratives of explorers generally waste few words on these Indians or the neighboring Paiute, classing them indiscriminately as "diggers" and dismissing them all with a few contemptuous words. They were affected materially by the discovery of the Comstock Lode. Although it was not in their territory, prospectors penetrated everywhere, stock was introduced which sorely affected the food supplies of the natives, and the resulting friction affected first the Northern Paiute and somewhat later the Shoshoni. Steward says:

By 1865, Shoshoni of Battle Mountain and Austin were involved. Meanwhile south of the Great Salt Lake in Utah and in eastern California, Shoshoni, especially those known as Gosiute, were committing depredations against immigrants, raiding the pony express and attacking the stage line which ran through this territory. . . . For protection, Fort Ruby in Ruby Valley was built in 1862. . . . An army unit massacred a large number of Shoshoni in Steptoe Valley in 1862, but by 1865 the strife was ended. In 1869 the railroad across the continent was completed and the native period was at an end. Shoshoni of central Nevada and of the more remote valleys seem to have kept pretty well out of the conflict. The treaty of 1863 included all the Shoshoni of northern Nevada. They were given the Western Shoshone or Duck Valley Reservation in 1877 (by Executive Order of April 16), but by no means all Shoshoni went to it. A few of the more westerly Shoshoni joined Paiute on reservations in western Nevada, but most Shoshoni remained near their native haunts, gradually abandoning their native economy and attaching themselves to ranches or mining towns. (Steward, 1938, p. 7.)

The Carlin Farms Reservation northwest of Elko was set aside by Executive Order of May 10, 1877, but restored to the public domain by Executive Order of January 16, 1879.

Population.—Mooney (1938) estimated that there were 4,500 Northern and Western Shoshoni together in 1845. The United States Census of 1910 gave 3,840, a figure which included about 1,800 Western Shoshoni. The United States Indian Office Report for 1917 indicated perhaps 1,500. The census of 1930 raised this figure into the neighborhood of 2,000, but in 1937 the Indian Office returned only 1,201.

Skitswish. From their own name; significance unknown. Also called:

Coeur d'Alêne, a French appellation meaning "awl heart," said to have been used originally by a chief to indicate the size of a trader's heart.
Q'ma'shpăl, Yakima name, meaning "camas people."
Pointed Hearts, derived from the word Coeur d'Alêne.

Connections.—The Skitswish belonged to the inland division of the Salishan stock, their closest relatives being the Kalispel or Pend d'Oreilles, and other eastern tribes.

Location.—On the headwaters of Spokane River from a little above Spokane Falls to the sources, including Coeur d'Alêne Lake and all its tributaries, and the head of the Clearwater.

Subdivisions and Villages

Teit (1930) reports the following divisions and villages, noting that the last in reality may have included two sections, the Coeur d'Alêne Lake Division and the Spokane River Division:

St. Joe River Division:
- Ntcaamtsen (.ntcäa'mtsᴇn), at the confluence of the St. Joe and St. Maries Rivers.
- Stiktakeshen (.sti'q^{u}takᴇcᴇn?), near the mouth of St. Joe River, on the river, or nearby on the lake.
- Stotseawes (stotsᴇă̈wᴇs), on St. Joe River, at the place now called Fish Trap by the Whites.
- Takolks (ta'x.olks) (?), on upper Hangman's River, at a spring near the foot of the hill just south of De Smet.
- Tcatowashalgs (tcat'owacalgs), on St. Joe River a little above Stotseawes.
- Tcetishtasheshen (tcêti'ctacᴇcᴇn), probably on the lake, near the Stiktakeshen, on the north or east side, not far from the mouth of the river.

Coeur d'Alêne River Division:
- Athlkwarit (ałqwarit), at Harrison.
- Gwalit (gwa'lît), near the lake and close to Harrison.
- Hinsalut (hînsä'lut), on Coeur d'Alêne River a little above Smakegen.
- Kokolshtelps (qoqolc'têlps), a little above Nestagwast.
- Nalstkathlkwen (nalstqa'łχwᴇn), a little above Senshalemants.
- Neatskstem (ne'atsxstᴇm), on Coeur d'Alêne River a little above Athlkwarit.
- Nêstagwast (nest'a'gwast), at Black Lake, at a tributary river and lake here.
- Senshalemants (sᴇncä'lᴇmänts), a little above Hinsalut.
- Smakegen (sma'qᴇgen), at Medimont.
- Skwato (sk'wat'o'), at old mission.
- Tclatcalk (tcła'tcalxw), on Coeur d'Alêne Lake, close to the mouth of Coeur d'Alêne River.

Coeur d'Alêne Lake and Spokane River Division.
- Ntaken (nt'a'q'ᴇn) Hayden Lake), north of Coeur d'Alêne Lake.
- Tcelatcelitcemen (tcêlätcelîtcᴇmᴇn), halfway down Coeur d'Alêne Lake, on the east side.
- Ntcemkainkwa (ntc'ᴇmqa'inqwa), at Coeur d'Alêne City.
- Smethlethlena (smᴇłᴇłe'na), near the last on the same side.
- Tpoenethlpem, very near the preceding, on the same side.

877646—52——27

Nsharept (ncā'rEpt), a little below the next to the last.
Stcatkwei (stcatkwe'i), a little below the last.
Kamilen (q'ămi'len), at Post Falls.
Hinsaketpens (hinsaq'a'tpEns), about one mile above the Spokane bridge.
Newashalks (ne'Ewa'calqs), a little below the preceding.
Ntsetsawolsako (ntsetsakwolsa'ko?), on Tamarack Creek, toward the mountains.
Neshwahwe (nesxwa'xxwe), on the river a little below the last two.
Nesthlihum (nesłi'xum), a little below the last.
Tcanokwaken (tcanokwā'kEn?), a little below the last.
Mulsh (mu'lc), at Green Acres.
Tcatenwahetpem (tcatenwa'x̣etpEm), a short distance below Green Acres, and about 20 miles above Spokane City.

History.—There is no tradition of any Skitswish migrations. Like so many other tribes in the region, the Skitswish were first brought clearly to the attention of Whites by Lewis and Clark. Although suffering the usual heavy losses following contact with Europeans, they continued to live in the same country and were finally allotted a reservation there bearing their name.

Population.—Mooney (1928) estimated that the Skitswish may have numbered 1,000 in 1780, but Teit (1930) raises this to from 3,000 to 4,000. In 1905 the United States Indian Office returned 494, all on the one reservation. The census of 1910 gave 293, probably below the true figure, as the United States Indian Office reported 601 on the reservation, including probably some Spokane, and in 1937 it returned 608.

Connections in which they have become noted.—Coeur d'Alêne Lake in northern Idaho and a town on its shores preserve the memory of the Skitswish, as they bear the name given this tribe by the French.

Snakes, see **Paiute, Northern.**

Spokan. The Spokan extended a few miles into this State along its western boundary. (See Washington.)

WASHINGTON

The State of Washington was occupied by a great number of Indian tribes formerly very populous, particularly those along the coast. There are few traditions regarding migrations and those which we have apply almost entirely to the interior people. After the Whites came it was unlikely that the Indians would move eastward in the face of the invasion and impossible for them to move westward; hence we do not have to trace various stages of long migrations due to displacement by the Whites and the overland retreat which followed, so marked in the history of the eastern Indians. Contrary to an older view, which held that Salishan tribes formerly extended to the lower Columbia and were driven north by Shahaptians, pushed forward in turn by Shoshonean peoples, it seems that the relative positions of Salishans and Shahaptians has been unchanged for an uncertain period of time and that, as a matter of fact, the Shoshoneans have been pushed southward although this movement was very recent. The Athapascan Kwalhioqua must represent a comparatively late invasion although that may not have been so recent as their anomalous position would lead one to suppose. There is also evidence of a much earlier movement when the Salishans came down upon the coast. The earliest European to meet any of the peoples of Washington was probably Juan de Fuca, a Greek navigator sailing under the Spanish flag, who, in 1592, visited the straits which now bear his name. Other Spanish explorers followed, and were later succeeded by English and Americans. The continual resort of trading vessels to Nootka on the west coast of Vancouver Island served to distribute European commodities and had a considerable influence among the tribes of Washington. In the latter part of the eighteenth century traders of the Hudson Bay and Northwest Companies made their appearance, but the Washington peoples first come squarely out upon the stage of history with the descent of the Columbia by Lewis and Clark in 1805–6. These pioneers gave the first general description of the region, enumerated the aboriginal peoples found in occupancy, and attempted estimates of their numbers. For some time afterward the territory was dominated by representatives of British companies and the land was claimed by England, while the only attempt to exploit it on the part of Americans, the settlement of Astoria, was soon abandoned. Following upon the acceptance of the 49th parallel of latitude as the International Boundary, however, and still more the discovery of gold in California and the opening up of the "Oregon trail," settlers from the Eastern States began to pour in in numbers. It was thereafter inevitable that friction should develop between the newcomers and the aborigines. There were wars with the Nez Percé, Yakima, and other tribes, but the Indians suffered less in this way than from European diseases, particularly the smallpox, which began their ravages before Lewis and Clark appeared, from spirituous liquors, and from a general dislocation of their aboriginal adjustments. The destruction was greatest in the Columbia Valley, which as the main artery of travel and trade was peculiarly exposed to epidemics, and within a few years the greater part of the once teeming populations of the lower valley were practically wiped out of existence. Roman Catholic missions sprang up at an early date in the eastern part of the territory, and were soon followed by those of Protestant denominations, notable among which was that conducted among the Cayuse by Marcus Whitman (1838–47). As in other parts of the United States, the Indians gradually parted with their lands and were placed upon reservations, though in most cases they were not removed so far from their original homes as in the eastern parts of the Union.

The above sketch will show enough of the history of most of the tribes in this area, though some details have been added in certain cases (i. e., in connection with the Cayuse, Chilluckittequaw, Chimakum, Chinook, Klickitat, and Yakima. (See Ray, 1932, and Spier and Sapir, 1930.)

Cathlamet. Significance unknown. Also called:

Guasámas, or Guithlamethl, by the Clackamas.
Kathlamet, own name.
Kwillu'chini, by the Chinook.

Connections.—The Cathlamet belonged to the Chinookan stock. The dialect to which they have given their name was spoken as far up the Columbia River as Ranier.

Location.—On the south bank of Columbia River near its mouth, claiming the territory between Tongue Point and the neighborhood of Puget Island, and on the north bank from the mouth of Grays Bay to a little east of Oak Point.

Villages

Ika'naiak, on the north side of the Columbia River at the mouth of Coal Creek Slough just east of Oak Point.

Ilo'humin, on the north side of Columbia River opposite Puget Island and near the mouth of Alockman Creek.

Kathla'amat, on the south side of Columbia River about 4 miles below Puget Island.

Ta'nas ilu', on Tanas Ilahee Island on the south side of the Columbia River.

Wa'kaiyakam, across Alockman Creek opposite Ilo'humin.

Population.—Mooney (1928) estimated 450 Cathlamet in 1780. In 1805–6 Lewis and Clark gave 300. In 1849 Lane reported 58. They are now extinct as a separate group.

Connection in which they have become noted.—The capital of Wahkiakum County, Washington, perpetuates the name of the Cathlamet.

Cathlapotle. Meaning "people of Lewis (Na'p!ōʟx.) River."

Connections.—The Cathlapotle belonged to the Chinookan linguistic stock and were placed by Spier (1936) in the Clackamas division of Upper Chinook but by Berreman (1937) apparently with the Multnomah.

Location.—On the lower part of Lewis River and the southeast side of the Columbia River, in Clarke County.

Villages

The main village of the Cathlapotle was Nahpooitle, at the mouth of Lewis River, but to this should perhaps be added Wakanasisi, opposite the mouth of Willamette River.

Population.—Mooney (1928) estimated 1,300 Cathlapotle in 1780; Lewis and Clark, 900 in 1806.

Connection in which they have become noted.—Lewis River was once known by the name of Cathlapotle.

Cayuse. The Cayuse were located about the heads of Wallawalla, Umatilla, and Grande Ronde Rivers, extending from the Blue Mountains to Deschutes River, Washington and Oregon. (See Oregon.)

Chehalis. Meaning "sand," the name derived originally, according to Gibbs (1877), from a village at the entrance of Grays Harbor. Also called:

Atchiχe'lish, Calapooya name.
Ilga't, Nestucca name.
Lower Chehalis, name used by Spier (1927).
Staq-tûbc, Puyallup name.

Connections.—The Chehalis belonged to the coastal division of the Salishan linguistic family, being most intimately related to the Humptulips, Wynoochee, and Quinault.

Location.—On the lower course of Chehalis River, especially on the south side, and on the south side of Grays Bay. In later times the Chehalis occupied territory to and about Willapa Bay that had formerly been held by the Chinook.

Villages

Chehalis (Gibbs, 1877), on the south side of Grays Harbor near Westport, in country earlier occupied by the Chinook.

Chiklisilkh (Gibbs), at Point Leadbetter, Willapa Bay, in territory earlier occupied by Chinook.

Hlakwun (Curtis, 1907–9), near Willapa on Willapa River in territory earlier occupied by the Chinook.

Kaulhlak (Curtis), at the head of Palux River, earlier in Chinook country.

Klumaitumsh (Gibbs and Boas personal information), given doubtfully as the name of a former band or village on the south side of Grays Harbor at its entrance.

Nai'yasap (Curtis), on Willapa River in territory earlier occupied by Chinook.

Nickomin (Swan 1857 and Boas, personal information), on North River which flows into Willapa Bay, in territory earlier occupied by the Chinook.

Noohooultch (Gibbs), on the south side of Grays Harbor.

Noosiatsks (Gibbs), on the south side of Grays Harbor.

Nooskoh (Gibbs), on a creek opposite Whishkah River.

Qyan (Gairdner, 1841), on the north point of Grays Harbor.

Talal (Gibbs), at Ford's Prairie on the Chehalis River near Centralia, and therefore far outside of the Chehalis territory proper.

Willapa, on Willapa River and in earlier Chinook country.

The following villages were originally occupied by Chinook but seem to have shifted in population or language or both so as to become Chehalis: Hwa'hots, Nutskwethlso'k, Quela'ptonlilt, Quer'quelin, Tske'lsos.

Population.—Mooney (1928) estimated a population of 1,000 in the year 1780 for the Lower and Upper Chehalis, the Cowlitz, the Humptulips, and related tribes, but the number had sunk to 170 by 1907. However, the census of 1910 gives 282 for the same group exclusive of the Cowlitz. In 1923 the United States Indian Office returned 89, and in 1937, 131.

Connections in which they have become noted.—A river, county, and city in Washington preserve the name of the Chehalis. There is a Chehalis in Minnesota but its name probably has no connection with that of the Washington tribe.

Chelan. The name is derived from Chelan Lake.

Connections.—An interior Salish tribe speaking the Wenachee dialect and separated tentatively from that tribe by Spier (1927).

Location.—At the outlet of Lake Chelan.

Population.—No data.

Connections in which they have become noted.—The name Chelan is shared not only by the lake above mentioned but by Chelan Falls, a range of mountains, a county, and two post villages, Chelan and Chelan Falls.

Chilluckittequaw. Significance unknown.

Connections.—The Chilluckittequaw belonged to the Chinookan linguistic stock.

Location.—As reported by Lewis and Clark, the Chilluckittequaw lay along the north side of Columbia River, in the present Klickitat and Skamania Counties, from about 10 miles below the Dalles to the neighborhood of the Cascades. Spier (1936) thinks they may have been identical with the White Salmon or Hood River group of Indians and perhaps both. In the latter case we must suppose that they extended to the south side of the Columbia.

Subdivisions and Villages

Itkilak or Ithlkilak (occupied jointly with Klickitat), at White Salmon Landing.

Nanshuit (occupied jointly with Klickitat), at the present Underwood.

Smackshop, a band of Chilluckittequaw extending from the River Labiche (Hood River ?) to the Cascades.

Tgasgutcu (occupied jointly with Klickitat), said to be about ½ mile west of a long, high mountain opposite Mosier, Oreg., and at the same time about a mile above White Salmon Landing, an apparent inconsistency.

Thlmieksok or Thlmuyaksok, ½ mile from the last; in 1905 the site of the Burket Ranch.

Historical Note.—According to Mooney (1928), a remnant of the Chilluckittequaw lived near the mouth of the White Salmon River until 1880 when they removed to the Cascades, where a few still resided in 1895.

Population.—Mooney (1928) estimated 3,000 for this tribe in 1780. In 1806 Lewis and Clark placed the figure at 1,400, besides 800 Smackshop, or a total of 2,200.

Chimakum. Significance of the name is unknown. Also called:

Aqokúlo, own name.
Port Townsend Indians, popular name.

Connections.—The Chimakum, the Quileute, and the Hoh (q. v.) together constituted the Chimakuan linguistic stock, which in turn was probably connected with the Salishan stock.

Location.—On the peninsula between Hood's Canal and Port Townsend.

History.—The Chimakum were constantly at war with the Clallam and other Salish tribes and, being inferior in numbers, suffered very much at their hands. They were included in the Point-no-Point Treaty of 1855 and placed on the Skokomish Reservation, where they gradually diminished in numbers until, in 1890, Boas was able to find only three individuals who could speak their language, and then but imperfectly.

Population.—Mooney (1928) estimates 400 Chimakum in 1780, and Gibbs (1877), 90 in 1855. The census of 1910 enumerated 3.

Connection in which they have become noted.—Attention was called to the Chimakum in early days by their warlike character and the uniqueness of their language.

Chinook. From Tsinúk, their Chehalis name. Also called:

Ala'dshūsh, Nestucca name.
Flatheads, a name shared with a number of other tribes in the region from their custom of deforming the head.
Thlála'h, Clackama name.

Connections.—The Chinook belonged to the Lower Chinook division of the Chinookan family.

Location.—On the north side of the Columbia River from its mouth to Grays Bay (not Grays Harbor), a distance of about 15 miles, and north along the seacoast to include Willapa or Shoalwater Bay. Ray (1938) makes a separate division to include the Shoalwater Chinook but it will be more convenient to treat them under one head. It is understood that they differed not at all in dialect.

Towns

(As given by Ray (1938), except as otherwise indicated)

Clamoitomish (Sapir, 1930), in Grays Bay.
Hakelsh, at the mouth of Smith Creek on the northeast shore of Willapa Bay.
Hwa'hots, at a former settlement called Bruceport about 3 miles north of the mouth of Palix River.
Ini'sal, on Naselle River where it enters the arm of Willapa Bay.
Iwa'lhat, at the mouth of Wallicut River, which bears its name in a corrupted form.
Kalawa'uus, on the peninsula at Oysterville Point.
Killaxthokle (Lewis and Clark, 1905–6), probably on Willapa Bay.
Kwatsa'mts, on Baker Bay at the mouth of Chinook River, north side of the Columbia.
Lapi'lso, on an island in an arm of Willapa Bay below the mouth of Naselle River.
Ma'hu, at the mouth of Nemah River below the present town of Nemah.
Mo'kwal, at the mouth of Deep River on Grays Bay.
Nahume'nsh, on the west side of North River at its mouth on the north shore of Willapa Bay.
Namla'iks, at Goose Point.
Na'mstcats, at a site now called Georgetown between Tokeland and North Cove.
Nokska'itmithls, at Fort Canby on Cape Disappointment.
No'skwalakuthl, at Ilwaco, named after its last chief.
Nu'kaunthl, at Tokeland, named after its chief.
Nu'patstcthl, at the site of Nahcotta, on the peninsula opposite the mouth of Nemah River.
Nutskwethlso'k, on Willapa Bay west of Bay Center.
Nuwi'lus, on the site of Grayland on the coast.
Quela'ptonlilt (Swan, 1857), at the mouth of Willapa River.
Querquelin (Swan), at the mouth of Querquelin River, which flows into Palix River from the south near the mouth of the latter.
Se'akwal, on the north bank of the Columbia a short distance below Mo'kwal.
Tokpi'luks, at the mouth of Palix River.
Tse'yuk, at Oysterville on the peninsula north of Nahcotta.
Tske'lsos, on Willapa River between South Bend and Raymond.
Ya'kamnok, at Sandy Point 3 miles south of Goose Point, the extreme north point at Bay Center.

History.—Though the Chinook had been known to traders for an indefinite period previously, they were first described by Lewis and Clark, who visited them in 1805. From their proximity to Astoria and their intimate relations with the early traders, they soon became well known, and their language formed the chief Indian basis for the Chinook jargon, first employed as a trade language, which ultimately extended from California to Alaska. In the middle of the nineteenth century they became mixed with the Chehalis with whom they ultimately fused entirely, dropping their own language. The Chinook of later census returns are composed of a number of other tribes of the same stock.

Population.—Mooney (1928) estimates that there were 800 of these Indians in 1780, "including the Chinook and Killaxthokl." In 1805 Lewis and Clark gave 400 on Columbia River alone. In 1885 Swan states that there were 112. They are now nearly extinct though Ray (1938) discovered three old people still living as late as 1931-36.

Connection in which they have become noted.—The name of the Chinook tribe became famous (1) because of intimate dealings between the Chinook and British and American traders, (2) on account of the extension of their name to the related tribes now classed in the Chinookan stock, (3) because the name was also extended to the Chinook jargon or Oregon Trade Language known throughout the entire Northwest, (4) because of its application to the Chinook or Pacific wind, and (5) from its application to towns in Pacific County, Wash., and Blaine County, Mont.

Clackamas. Placed on both sides of the Columbia, but I prefer to follow Berreman (1937) in limiting the term to groups living on the Oregon side. (See Oregon.)

Clallam. Meaning "strong people." Also spelled Nu-sklaim, S'Klallam, Tla'lem.

Connections.—The Clallam were a tribe of the coastal division of the Salishan linguistic stock most closely connected with the Songish.

Location.—On the south side of the Strait of Juan de Fuca, between Port Discovery and Hoko River. Later the Clallam occupied the Chimakum territory also and a small number lived on the lower end of Vancouver Island.

Villages

Elwah, at the mouth of Elwah River.
Hoko, at the mouth of Hoko Creek.
Huiauulch, on the site of modern Jamestown, 5 miles east of Dungeness.
Hunnint or Hŭngĭ'ngĭt, on the east side of Clallam Bay; this town and Klatlawas together were called Xainañt by Erna Gunther (1927).
Kahtai, at Port Townsend, occupied after the destruction of the Chimakum.
Kaquaith (or Skakwiyel), at Port Discovery.
Klatlawas, the Tlătlăwai'is of Curtis (1907-9), on the west side of Clallam Bay; see Hunnint.
Kwahamish, a fishing village on the Lyre River.
Mekoŏs, on Beecher Bay, Vancouver Island, B. C.
Pistchin, on Pysht Bay.
Sequim or Suktcikwiiñ, on Sequim Bay or Washington Harbor.
Sestietl, Upper Elwah.
Stehtlum, at new Dungeness.
Tclanuk, on Beecher Bay, Vancouver Island, B. C.
Tsako, at the former mouth of Dungeness River.
Tsewhitzen, on Port Angeles Spit, 2 or 3 miles west of the old town of Stehtlum.
Yennis, at Port Angeles or False Dungeness.

Population.—Mooney (1928) estimated 2,000 Clallam in 1780. In 1854 Gibbs estimated 800. In 1855, 926 were reported. In 1862 Eells estimated 1,300 but gave 597 in 1878. In 1881 he reduced this to 485. In 1904, 336 were returned. By the census of 1910, 398 were reported; by the United States Indian Office in 1923, 535, and in 1937, 764.

Connections in which they have become noted.—The name Clallam is perpetuated by its application to a bay, a county, a river, and a precinct in the State of Washington.

Clalskanie. (See Oregon.)

Columbia or **Sinkiuse-Columbia.** So called because of their former prominent association with Columbia River, where some of the most important bands had their homes. Also called:

Bō'tcaced, by the Nez Percé, probably, meaning "arrows" or "arrow people."
Isle-de-Pierre, a traders' name, perhaps from a place in their country or for a band of the tribe.
Middle Columbia Salish, so called by Teit (1928) and Spier (1930 b).
Papspê'lu, Nez Percé name, meaning "firs," or "fir-tree people."
.sa'ładebc, probably the Snohomish name.
Sinkiuse, the name applied to themselves and most other neighboring Salish tribes, and said to have belonged originally and properly to a band which once inhabited Umatilla Valley.
Suwa'dabc, Snohomish name for all interior Indians, meaning "inland people," or "interior people."
.swā'dab.c, Twana name for all interior Indians, meaning "inland people."
.swa'namc, Nootsak name for all interior Indians, meaning "inland people."
Ti'attłuxa, Wasco Chinook name.
.tskowā'xtsᴇnux or .skowa'xtsᴇnᴇx, applied by themselves, meaning has something to do with "main valley."

Connections.—The Sinkiuse-Columbia belonged to the inland division of the Salishan linguistic stock, their nearest relatives being the Wenatchee and Methow.

Subdivisions or Bands

(According to Teit, 1930)

.nkeē'us or .s.nkeiē'usox (Umatilla Valley).
Stata'ketux, around White Bluffs on the Columbia.
.tskowā'xtsᴇnux or .skowa'xtsᴇnᴇx, also called Moses-Columbia or Moses Band after a famous chief (Priest's Rapids and neighboring country).

Curtis (1907–9) gives the following: "Near the mouth of the sink of Crab Creek were the Sĭnkŭmkŭnătkuh, and above them the Sĭnkolkolumĭnuh. Then came in succession the Stapĭ'sknuh, the Skukulăt'kuh, the Skoáhchnuh, the Skĭhlkĭntnuh, and, finally, the Skultaqchĭ'mh, a little above the mouth of Wenatchee River." Spier (1927) adds that the Sinkowarsin met by Thompson in 1811 might have been a band of this tribe.

Location and History.—The Sinkiuse-Columbia lived on the east side of Columbia River from Fort Okanogan to the neighborhood of Point Eaton. Later a reservation was created for them known as Columbia Reservation. In 1870 Winans placed them "on the east and south sides of the Columbia River from the Grand Coulée down to Priest's Rapids." They are now under the jurisdiction of Colville Agency and one band, the Moses-Columbia Band, is in the southern part of Colville Reservation.

Population.—The Sinkiuse-Columbia are estimated by Mooney (1928) to have numbered 800 in 1780, but were probably considerably more numerous as Teit (1927) considers that this tribe and the Pisquow together must have totaled something like 10,000 before the smallpox reached them. In 1905, 355 were reported; in 1908, 299; and in 1909, perhaps including some others, 540 were returned. The census of 1910 gave 52.

Colville. The name is derived from Fort Colville, a post of the Hudson's Bay Company at Kettle Falls, which was in turn named for the London governor of the company at the time when the post was founded, i. e., in 1825. Also called:

Basket People, by Hale (1846).
Chaudière, French name derived from the popular term applied to them, Kettle Falls Indians.
Kettle Falls Indians, as above.
Sălsχuyilp, Okanagon name.
Skuyélpi, by other Salish tribes.
Whe-el-po, by Lewis and Clark, shortened from above.

Connections.—The Colville belonged to the inland division of the Salishan linguistic stock and to that branch of the latter which included the Okanagon, Sanpoil, and Senijextee.

Location.—On Colville River and that part of the Columbia between Kettle Falls and Hunters.

Villages and Subdivisions

(From Ray, 1932)

Kakalapia, home of the Skakalapiak (across from the present town of Harvey, at the point where the ferry now crosses).
Kilumaak, home of the Skilumaak (opposite the present town of Kettle Falls, about 1½ miles above Nchumutastum).
Nchaliam, home of the Snchalik (about 1½ miles above the present town of Inchelium).
Nchumutastum, home of the Snchumutast (about 6 miles above Nilamin).
Nilamin, home of the Snilaminak (about 15 miles above Kakalapia).
Nkuasiam, home of the Snkuasik (slightly above the present town of Daisy, on the opposite side of the river).
Smichunulau, home of the Smichunulauk (at the site of the present State bridge at Kettle Falls).

History.—The history of the Colville was similar to that of the neighboring tribes except that Kettle Falls was early fixed upon as the site of an important post by the Hudson Bay Company and brought with it the usual advantages and disadvantages of White contact.

Population.—Mooney (1928) estimated the number of the Colville at 1,000 as of 1780, but Lewis and Clark placed it at 2,500, a figure also fixed upon by Teit (1930). In 1904 there were 321; in 1907, 334; and in 1937, 322.

Connections in which they have become noted.—The name Colville was applied to an important Indian Reservation and later to a town, the county seat of Stevens County, Wash., but the original, of course, was not Indian.

Copalis. Significance unknown.

Connections.—The Copalis belonged to the coastal division of the Salishan linguistic family.

Location.—Copalis River and the Pacific Coast between the mouth of Joe Creek and Grays Harbor.

Population.—Lewis and Clark in 1805 estimated a population of 200 Copalis in 10 houses. The 5 individuals assigned to a "Chepalis" tribe in an enumeration given by Olson of the year 1888 probably refers to them.

Connections in which they have become noted.—The name Copalis is perpetuated in that of Copalis River, and in the post villages of Copalis Beach and Copalis Crossing, Grays Harbor County, Wash.

Cowlitz. Significance unknown. Also called:

Nū-sō-lupsh, name given by Indians not on the Sound to Upper Cowlitz and Upper Chehalis.

Connections.—The Cowlitz belonged to the coastal division of the Salishan linguistic family, yet shared some peculiarities with the inland tribes.

Location.—Most of the lower and all the middle course of Cowlitz River. Later they were divided between Chehalis and Puyallup Reservations.

Towns

Ray (1932) gives: Awi'mani, at the mouth of Coweman River, south of Kelso, and Manse'la, on site of Longiew. (See Curtis, 1907–9.)

Population.—Mooney (1928) estimated the number of the Cowlitz, along with the Chehalis, Humptulips, and some other tribes, at 1,000 in 1780. In 1853 Gibbs stated that they and the Upper Chehalis counted not more than 165. About 1887 there were 127 on Puyallup Reservation. The census of 1910 returned 105. The United States Indian Office Report of 1923 gives 490, probably including other tribes.

Connections in which they have become noted.—The name Cowlitz is perpetuated by Cowlitz River and Cowlitz Pass; by Cowlitz Glacier, which radiates from Mount Ranier; and by Cowlitz County, Cowlitz

Park, Cowlitz Chimney, Cowlitz Cleaver, and some small towns in the same region.

Duwamish. A place name.

Connections.—The Duwamish belonged to the Nisqually dialectic group of the coast division of the Salishan linguistic stock.

Subdivisions and Villages

(According to Smith, 1940)

A. The Duwamish River from its mouth up to and including the Black and Cedar Rivers, with the following villages:
Dsidsila'letc, at Yesler Way and Jackson St., Seattle.
Duwe'kwulsh, at Maple Valley.
Kati'lbabsh, at the present town of Renton.
Sakwe'kwewad, on Cedar River about 2 miles from Renton.
Skwa'lko, where the Black and White Rivers join to form the Duwamish.
Tkwabko', at south end of Lake Washington.
Tola'ltu, below Duwamish Head, Seattle.
Tupa'thlteb, at the mouth of the easternmost estuary of the Duwamish.
Tuduwa'bsh, at the mouth of the Duwamish River.

B. From where the Black River flows into the Duwamish to the junction of the White and Green Rivers, including these villages:
Stak and Tcutupa'lhu, on the east bank of the White River between its junction with the Black River and the mouth of the Green River.

C. The Green River villages:
Ila'lkoabsh, at the junction of the Green and White Rivers.
Su'sabsh, on Suise Creek.
Perhaps several groups of houses: (1) on the upper Green River, including Tskoka'bid (at the bend now spanned by the highway bridge about 4 miles east of Auburn); (2) on the north bank of the Robert Wooding Place; (3) on the Du Bois Place, and (4) at the mouth of Newaukum Creek.

D. The White River village, Sbalko'absh (on White River near a small stream at the southeast corner of the present Muckleshoot Reservation and to the east on Boise Creek).

E. The Lake Washington people, including the Thluwi'thalbsh (at Union Bay), the Sammamish (at the mouth of Sammamish River), and the peoples of Salmon Bay. In 1856 they were removed to the eastern shore of Bainbridge Island but as the place lacked a fishing ground they were shortly afterward taken to Holderness Point, on the west side of Eliot Bay, which was already a favorite place for fishing. They are now under the Tulalip School Superintendency.

Population.—The Duwamish were estimated by Mooney (1928), with the Suquamish and other tribes, at 1,200 in 1780. About 1856 they are variously given at from 64 to 312. The census of 1910 returned 20.

Connections in which they have become noted.—The Duwamish will be remembered mainly as one of the tribes formerly located on the site of Seattle, and one of the two of which the Indian who gave his name to that city was chief. The name Duwamish itself is preserved in Duwamish River and in the name of a small town.

Hoh. Significance unknown.

Connections.—The Hoh spoke the Quileute language and were often considered part of the same tribe, constituting one division of the Chimakuan linguistic stock and more remotely connected with the Salishan family.

Location.—On Hoh River on the west coast of Washington.

Population.—Mooney (1928) estimates 500 in the Hoh and the Quileute together in 1780. In 1905 the Hoh numbered 62.

Connection in which they have become noted.—The name Hoh is preserved in that of the Hoh River.

Humptulips. Said to signify "chilly region."

Connections.—The Humptulips belonged to the coastal division of the Salishan linguistic stock, being connected most closely with the Chehalis.

Location.—On the Humptulips River, and part of Grays Harbor, including also Hoquiam Creek and Whiskam River.

Villages

Hli'mŭmi (Curtis, 1907–9), near North Cove.
Hoquiam, on Hoquiam Creek.
Hooshkal (Gibbs), on the north shore of Grays Harbor.
Kishkallen (Gibbs), on the north shore of Grays Harbor.
Klimmim (Gibbs), 1877).
Kplelch (Curtis), at the mouth of North River.
Kwapks (Curtis, 1907–9), at the mouth of North River.
Mo'nilŭmsh (Curtis), at Georgetown.
Nooachhummik (Gibbs), on the coast north of Grays Harbor.
Nookalthu (Gibbs), north of Grays Harbor.
Nu'moihanhl (Curtis), at Tokeland.
Whishkah, on Whishkah River.

These are placed under the Humptulips only on account of their locations as described.

Population.—See **Chehalis.** In 1888 according to Olsen 18 Humptulips were reported. In 1904 there were 21.

Connection in which they have become noted.—Humptulips River and a village in Grays Harbor County preserve the name of the Humptulips Indians.

Kalispel. The Kalispel extended over into the eastern edge of the State from Idaho (q. v.).

Klickitat. From a Chinook term meaning "beyond" and having reference to the Cascade Mountains. Also called:

Awi-adshi, Molala name.
Lûk'-a-tatt, Puyallup name.
Máhane, Umpqua name.
Mĭ-Çlauq'-tcu-wûn'-ti, Alsea name, meaning "scalpers."

Mûn-an′-nĕ-qu′ tûnnĕ, Naltunnetunne name, meaning "inland people."
Qwû′lh-hwai-pûm, own name, meaning "prairie people."
Tlakăĭ′tat, Okanagon name.
Tsĕ la′kayāt amím, Kalapuya name.
Tiuwānxa-ikc, Clatsop name.
Wahnookt, Cowlitz name.

Connections.—The Klickitat belonged to the Shahaptian division of the Shapwailutan linguistic family.

Subdivisions and Villages

Possibly the Atanum or Atanumlema should be added to the Klickitat. Mooney (1928) reports that their language was distinct from, though related to, both Klickitat and Yakima.

The following villages are mentioned:

Itkilak or Ithlkilak, at White Salmon Landing, which they occupied jointly with the Chilluckquittequaw.
Nanshuit (occupied jointly with the Chilluckquittequaw), at Underwood.
Shgwaliksh, not far below Memaloose Island.
Tgasgutcu (occupied jointly with the Chilluckquittequaw), said to be about ½ mile west of a long high mountain opposite Mosier, Oreg., and about 1 mile above White Salmon Landing but the exact location seems to be in doubt.
Wiltkun (exact location unknown).

History.—The original home of the Klickitat was somewhere south of the Columbia, and they invaded their later territory after the Yakima crossed the river. In 1805 Lewis and Clark found them wintering on Yakima and Klickitat Rivers. Taking advantage of the weakness of the Willamette tribes following upon an epidemic of fever between 1820 and 1830, the Klickitat crossed the Columbia and forced their way as far south as the valley of the Umpqua but were soon compelled to retire to their old seats. They were active and enterprising traders, profiting by their favorable location to become middlemen between the coast tribes and those living east of the Cascades. They joined in the Yakima treaty at Camp Stevens, June 9, 1855, by which they ceded their lands to the United States, and most of them settled upon the Yakima Reservation.

Population.—Mooney (1928) estimated that the Klickitat, including the Taitinapam, numbered 600 in 1780. In 1805 Lewis and Clark placed their total population at about 700. The census of 1910 returned 405

Connections in which they have become noted.—The Klickitat were early distinguished from other tribes of central Washington owing to their propensity for trading. The name is perpetuated in that of a small affluent of the Columbia and in the name of the county, and a post village in the county.

Kwaiailk. Meaning unknown. Also called:

Kwū-teh-ni, Kwalhioqua name.
Nū-sō-lupsh, by Sound Indians, referring to the rapids of their stream.
Stak-ta-mish, a name for this and other inland tribes, meaning "forest people."
Upper Chehalis, common name.

Connections.—The Kwaiailk belonged to the coastal division of the Salishan linguistic family but a part of them were associated with the inland tribes by certain peculiarities of speech. Their nearest relatives seem to have been the Cowlitz and Chehalis.

Location.—On the upper course of Chehalis River.

Subdivisions and Villages

Cloquallum, on Cloquallum River.

Population.—In 1855, according to Gibbs (1877), the Kwaiailk numbered 216 but were becoming amalgamated with the Cowlitz. (See **Chehalis.**)

Kwalhioqua. From their Chinook designation, meaning "a lonely place in the woods." Also called:

Axwē'lāpc, "people of the Willapa," by the Chinook and Quinault Indians.
Gilā'q!ulawas, from the name of the place where they usually lived.
Owhillapsh or Willapa, applied to this tribe erroneously.
Tkulhiyogoā'ikc, Chinook name.

Connections.—The Kwalhioqua belonged to the Athapascan linguistic stock.

Location.—On the upper course of Willopah River, and the southern and western headwaters of the Chehalis. Gibbs (1877) extends their territory eastward of the Cascades, but Boas (1892) doubts the correctness of this.

Subdivisions

Suwal, on headwaters of the Chehalis.
Wela'pakote'li, on Willapa River.

Population.—Mooney (1928) estimated 200 in 1780; Hale (1846) gives about 100, but in 1850 it is said that only 2 males and several females survived, which indicates that an error had been made by one or the other.

Connection in which they have become noted.—The Kwalhioqua were distinguished almost solely by the fact that they belonged to the great Athapascan group yet were the only tribe of that stock in the State of Washington in historic times, having become entirely isolated from their relatives.

Lummi. Significance unknown. Also spelled Hâ-lum-mi, Nuh-lum-mi, and Qtlumi. Also called:

Nūkhlésh, by the Skagit, who also included the Clallam in the designation.

Connections.—The Lummi belonged to the coastal division of the Salishan linguistic family and spoke, according to Boas (1911), the same dialect as the Songish of Vancouver Island.

Location.—On the upper part of Bellingham Bay and about the mouth of Nooksack River. Formerly the Lummi are said to have resorted at times to a group of islands east of Vancouver Island. They were finally placed on Lummi Reservation.

Villages

(According to Stern, 1934)

Elek, near the upper end of Bellingham Bay.
Hwetlkiem, near the upper end of Bellingham Bay west of Nooksack River.
Kwakas, on the north side of Nooksack River.
Momli, near the mouth of Nooksack River.
Skalisan, north of Point Francis and opposite Lummi Island.

The following fishing stations are also cited:

Hoholos, a point on Orcas Island south of Freeman Island.
Hwitcosang, in Upright Channel south of Shaw Island.
Hwtcihom or Bee Station, north of Sandy Point.
Skalekushan or Village Point, on Lummi Island.
Skoletc, on Lopez Island opposite Lopez.
Tceltenem, Point Roberts.
Tlkwoloks, on Orcas Island.

Population.—Mooney (1928) estimates the number of Lummi at 1,000 in 1780, including the Samish and Nooksack. In 1905 there were 412; according to the census of 1910, 353; according to the United States Indian Office Report for 1923, 505; and according to that for 1937, 661.

Connection in which they have become noted.—Lummi River, Washington, preserves the name.

Makah. Meaning "cape people." Also called:

Ba-qa-ǒ, Puyallup name.
Cape Flattery Indians, from their location.
Classet, Nootka name, meaning "outsiders."
Kwe-nēt-che-chat, own name, meaning "cape people."
Tlā'asath, Nootka name, meaning "outside people."

Connections.—The Makah belonged to the Nootka branch of the Wakashan linguistic family.

Location.—About Cape Flattery, claiming the coast east as far as Hoko River and south to Flattery Rocks, besides Tatoosh Island. Later they were confined to the Makah Reservation.

Villages

Winter towns:
- Baada, on Neah Bay.
- Neah, on the site of the old Spanish fort, Port Nuñez Gaona, Neah Bay.
- Waatch, at the mouth of Waatch Creek, 4 miles from Neah Bay.

Summer villages:
- Ahchawat, at Cape Flattery.
- Kehsidatsoos, location unknown.
- Kiddekubbut, 3 miles from Neah Bay.
- Tatooche, on Tatoosh Island, off Cape Flattery.

Population.—Together with the Ozette, the Makah were estimated by Mooney (1928) to number 2,000 in 1780, a figure evidently based on that given by Lewis and Clark in 1805. In 1905 there were 435; the census of 1910 gave 360, and the United States Indian Office Report for 1923 gave 425, including the people of Ozette. In 1937, 407 were returned besides the Ozette Indians.

Connection in which they have become noted.—The Makah and the Ozette are peculiar as the only tribes of the Nootka group and the Wakashan stock in the United States.

Methow. Meaning unknown. The Battle-le-mule-emauch of Ross (1847, p. 290).

Connections.—The Methow spoke a dialect belonging to the interior division of the Salishan linguistic stock.

Location.—On Methow River. A detached band called Chilowhist wintered on the Okanogan River between Sand Point and Malott.

Population.—Mooney (1928) estimated that this band and the Columbia Indians, or rather Moses' band of Columbia Indians, numbered 800 in 1780. In 1907 there were 324.

Connection in which they have become noted.—Methow River and Valley and a post village perpetuate the name of the Methow Indians.

Mical. Significance unreported.

Connections.—The Mical were a branch of the Shahaptian tribe called Pshwanwapam.

Location.—On the upper course of Nisqually River.

Population.—No separate data.

Muckleshoot. From the native word o'kelcuł, significance unknown.

Connections.—The Muckleshoot belonged to the Nisqually dialectic group of the coastal division of the Salishan linguistic family.

Location.—On White River, their territory extending from Kent eastward to the mountains, but it seems also to have included Green River.

Subdivisions

The following names appear applied to bands in their territory:

Sekamish, on White River.
Skopamish, on upper Green River.
Smulkamish, on upper White River

Smith (1940) adds Dothliuk, at South Prairie below where Cole Creek enters South Prairie Creek, an affluent of Carbon River.

Population.—The Muckleshoot are probably included in the 1,200 "Nisqually, Puyallup, etc." estimated by Mooney (1928) as in existence in 1780. The Skopamish numbered 222 in 1863 and the Smulkamish about 183 in 1870. Mooney estimated a total of 780 in 1907 for the group above given. In 1937 the United States Office of Indian Affairs reported 194 Indians of this tribe.

Connection in which they have become noted.—The name of the Muckleshoot is preserved in that of Muckleshoot Indian Reservation.

Neketemeuk. A supposed Salishan tribe placed by Teit's informants at an early period near and above the Dalles. Ray (1932), however, discredits the existence of an independent tribe of this name.

Nespelem, a division of the Sanpoil (q. v.).

Nez Percé. The Nez Percé occupied territory in the extreme southeastern part of the state. (See Idaho.)

Nisqually. From Skwale'absh, the native name of Nisqually River. Also spelled Quallyamish, and Skwalliahmish. Also called:

Askwalli, Calapooya name.
Ltsχe'als, Nestucca name.
Suketī'kenuk, Sukotī'kenuk, by Columbia Indians along with all other coast people, meaning "people of the other side," with reference to the Cascades.
Tsĕ Skua'lli ami'm, Luckamiut Kalapooian name.

Connections.—They gave their name to one dialectic division of the coastal division of the Salishan linguistic stock.

Location.—On Nisqually River above its mouth and on the middle and upper courses of Puyallup River.

Subdivisions and Villages

Basha'labsh, on Mashell Creek and neighboring Nisqually River, the town on a highland below Eatonville on Mashell Creek.
Sakwi'absh, Clear Creek and neighboring Nisqually River, the main settlement on a hill near the junction of Clear Creek and the Nisqually River.
Sigwa'letcabsh, on Segualitcu River, the main settlement where Dupont Creek enters the Sqwualitcu River.
Tsakwe'kwabsh, on Clarks Creek and neighboring Puyallup River, the main settlement where Clarks Creek empties into Puyallup River, but seems to have included also Skwa'dabsh, at the mouth of a creek entering Wappato Creek above the Wappato Creek village.
Sta'habsh, where the Stuck River enters the Puyallup.
Tsuwa'diabsh, on what is now the Puyallup River above its junction with the Carbon, and just below the site of the Soldiers' Home.
Tuwha'khabsh, above Ortig where Vogt Creek enters the Carbon River.
Yisha'ktcabsh, on Nisqually Lake, the principal settlement being at the mouth of a sizable creek.

Yokwa'lsshabsh, on Muck Creek and the neighboring parts of Nisqually River, the main settlement located where Muck Creek enters Nisqually River, and a division on Clover Creek.

Population.—Mooney (1928) estimated that in 1780 there were about 3,600 Nisqually of whom, in 1907, between 1,100 and 1,200 survived. About 1,100 were returned in the census of 1910, but the Indian Office Report for 1937 gives only 62, evidently a minor tribe which gave its name to the larger body.

Connection in which they have become noted.—The memory of the Nisqually tribe, or cluster of bands, has been preserved in the name of Nesqually or Nisqually River, and in the post village of Nisqually in Thurston County.

Nooksack. Meaning "mountain men." Also spelled Nooksak and Nootsak.

Connections.—The Nooksack belonged to the coastal division of the Salishan linguistic family. Hill-Tout (1902) says they separated from the Squawmish of British Columbia and speak the same dialect.

Location.—On Nooksack River, Whatcom County. (See also Canada.)

Population.—In 1906, 200 Nooksack were officially returned, but Hill-Tout (1902) states that in 1902 there were only about 6 true male members of the tribe. The census of 1910 gives 85 under this name, and the Report of the United States Office of Indian Affairs for 1937 returned 239. (See **Lummi.**)

Connection in which they have become noted.—Nooksack River and Nooksack town in Whatcom County, Washington, preserve the name.

Ntlakyapamuk. The southern bands of this tribe hunted over in the territory now embraced in Washington. (See Canada.)

Okanagon. From the native term Okanā'qēn, Okanāqē'nix, or Okinā'qēn. The name is derived from some place on the Okanogan River, near Okanogan Falls at the mouth of the Similkameen, where is said to have been the headquarters of a large band of the tribe and is even given as the place of origin of the entire tribe. Also called:

Akênuq'ḷā'lām or KōkEnu'k'kē, by Kutenai (Chamberlain, 1892).
Isonkuaĺli, own name, meaning "our people."
Kānk.'utḷā'atlam, Kutenai name, meaning "flatheads" (Boas, 1911).
KEnāke'n, by Tobacco Plains Band of Klickitat.
OtcEnāke', OtcEnā.qai'n, or UtcEnā'.qai'n, by the Salish and their allies.
Soo-wān'-a-mooh, Shuswap name.
.SoqEnāqai'mEX, Columbia name.
Tcutzwā'ut, Tcitxûā'ut, Tsawa'nEmux, or OkEnā.qai'n, Ntlakyapamuk names.
WEtc.nāqei'n, Skitswish name.

Connections.—The Okanagon belonged to the interior division of the Salishan stock, but their closest relatives were the Sanpoil, Colville, and Senijextee.

Location.—On Okanagan River above the mouth of the Similkameen to the Canadian border and in British Columbia along the shores of Okanagan Lake and in the surrounding country; in later times they have displaced an Athapascan tribe and part of the Ntlakyapamuk from the Similkameen Valley. (See also Canada.)

Subdivisions and Villages

The Similkameen Okanagon were divided into three bands, the Okanagon proper into four; with the villages belonging to each, they are as follows:

Upper Similkameen Band:

Ntkaihelok (Ntkai'xelôx), about 11 miles below Princeton, north side of Similkameen River.

Snazaist (Snäzäi'st), on the north shore of Similkameen River, a little east of Twenty-mile Creek and the town of Hedley.

Tcutcuwiha (Tcutcuwî'xa) or Tcutcawiha (Tcutcawī'xa), on the north side of Similkameen River, a little below the preceding.

Ashnola Band:

Ashnola (Acnū'lôx), on the south side of Similkameen River, near the mouth of Ashnola Creek.

Nsrepus (Nsre'pus) or Skanek, .sa'nEX, a little below the Ashnola, but on the north side of Similkameen River.

Lower Similkameen Band:

KekerEmyeaus (KekerEmyē'aus), across Similkameen River from Keremyeus.

Keremyeus (KerEmye'us), on the north side of Similkameen River, near Keremeos.

Nkura-elok (Nkuraē'lôx), on the south side of Similkameen River and about 4 miles below KerEmyeaus.

Ntleuktan (Ntleuxta'n), on the south side of Similkameen River, opposite Skemkain.

Skemkain (Skemquai'n), a short distance below Nkuraelok.

Smelalok (Smela'lox), on the south side of Similkameen River, about 10 miles below Nsrepus.

To the villages listed above must be added the following old Similkameen village sites in Washington:

Hepulok (Xe'pulôx).

Konkonetp (Ko'nkonetp), near the mouth of Similkameen River.

Kwahalos (Kwaxalo's), a little back from Similkameen River, below Hepulok.

Naslitok (Nā.sli'tok), just across the International Boundary in Washington.

Skwa'nnt, below Kwahalos.

Tsakeiskenemuk (Tsakei'sxEnEmux), on a creek along the trail between Keremeous and Penticton.

Tseltsalō's, below Kwahalos.

Douglas Lake Band:

Kathlemik (Kā.'lEmix), near Guichons, at the mouth of the Upper Nicola River, where it falls into Nicola Lake.

Komkonatko (Komkona'tko) or Komkenatk (KomkEna'tkk), at Fish Lake on the headwaters of the Upper Nicola River.

Kwiltcana (Kwiltca'na) at the mouth of Quilchene Creek.

Spahamen (Spā'xamEn) or Spahamen (Spā'xEmEn), at Douglas Lake.

Komaplix or Head of the Lake Band:

Nkamapeleks (Nkama'pElEks) or Nkomapeleks (Nkoma'pElEks), near the head of Okanagan Lake, about 8 miles north of Vernon.

Nkekemapeleks (Nkekema'pElEks), at the head of Long Lake, a little over a mile from Vernon.

Nkokosten (Nxok.o'stEn), a place near Kelowna, and also a general name for the district around there and Mission.

Skelaunna (SkElā'un.na), at Kelowna, near the present town.

Sntlemukten (SntlEmux̣te'n), (Black Town), a little north of the head of Okanagan Lake.

Stekatelkeneut (Stekatelx̣enē'ut), a little above Mission(?) on Long Lake opposite Tselotsus.

Tseketku (Tse'kEtku), at a small lake a little north of Black Town.

Tselotsus (TsElo'tsus), at the narrows of Long Lake.

Tskelhokem (TsxElho'qEm), near the lower end of Long Lake about 19 miles south of Vernon.

Penticton Band:

Penticton (Pentī'ktEn), Penticton, near the foot of Okanagan Lake.

Stekatkothlkneut (StEkatkoɫxne'ut) or Stekatethlkeneut (StEkatEɫxEnē'ut), on the opposite side of Long Lake from Mission.

Nkamip Band:

Nkamip (Nkamī'p), on the east side of the upper end of Osoyoos Lake.

Sci'yus, near Haynes or the old customhouse just north of the American line.

Skohenetk (Sx̣ox̣enē'tku[u]), at the lower end of Dog Lake.

To the villages listed above must be added the following names of old village sites on Okanagan River south of the Canadian line:

Milkemahituk (MilkEmaxi-tuk) or Milkemihituk (MilkEmixī'tuk), a general name for the district around the mouth of Similkameen River and of the river itself.

Okinaken (Ōkinā'qēn), an old name for Sathlilk.

Sathlilk (Saɫi'lx̣[u]), near the mouth of Similkameen River.

SmElkammin (Smelkammī'n), thought to be the old name of a place at the mouth of Similkameen River.

History.—The history of the Okanagon differed little from that of the Ntlakyapamuk and other neighboring tribes except that they were affected by the fact that a part of them were on the south side of the International Boundary. During the last two centuries, however, there has been a steady movement of the tribe northward, where they have displaced the Shuswap, who once hunted down to the head of Okanagan Lake and in the hinterland on the east side of it down to the latitude of Penticton. They have also displaced the Stuwik(?) and the Ntlakyapamuk in the Similkameen Valley.

Population.—Mooney (1928) estimated that there were about 2,200 Okanagon in 1780. Teit (1900) gives the population as between 2,500 and 3,000. In 1905, according to the Canadian and United States Departments of Indian Affairs, there were 1,516 Indians belonging to this tribe, including 824 in Canada and 692 in the United States. In 1906 the numbers were given as 824 and 527, respectively.

Connections in which they have become noted.—The name of the Okanagon in the form Okanogan has been given to a county, a town in that county, a precinct, and a river in the State of Washington, and in the form Okanagan to a lake and a town in British Columbia.

Ozette. Significance unknown.

Connections.—The Ozette were a southern branch of the Makah and belonged to the Nootka branch of the Wakashan linguistic family.

Location.—On the Ozette Lake and Ozette River in Clallam County.

Villages

Ozette, at Flattery Rocks.
Sooes, 4 miles south of the Makah village of Waatch.

Population.—(See **Makah**.) A single Ozette Indian was reported in 1937.

Connections in which they have become noted.—An island, a lake, a river, and a village are named Ozette after them.

Palouse. Significance unknown. Also called:

Pallotepellows, by Lewis and Clark in 1806.
.spalu'.sox̣, so called by Sinkiuse, said to be from a place name.

Connections.—The Palouse belonged to the Shahaptian division of the Shapwailutan linguistic stock, and were most closely connected with the Nez Percé.

Location.—In the valley of Palouse River in Washington and Idaho and on a small section of Snake River, extending eastward to the camas grounds near Moscow, Idaho. The Palouse were included in the Yakima treaty of 1855 but have never recognized the treaty obligations and have declined to lead a reservation life.

Subdivisions and Villages

Almotu, on the north bank of Snake River about 30 miles above the mouth of Palouse River.
Chimnapum, on the northwest side of Columbia River near the mouth of Snake River and on lower Yakima River.
Kasispa, at Ainsworth, at the junction of Snake and Columbia Rivers, Wash.
Palus, on the north bank of Snake River just below its junction with the Palouse.
Sokulk or Wanapum, on Columbia River above the mouth of Snake River.
Tasawiks, on the north bank of Snake River, about 15 miles above its mouth.

History.—The Palouse are said to have separated from the Yakima.

Population.—Estimated by Mooney (1928) at 5,400 in 1780. In 1805 Lewis and Clark gave 1,600. In 1854 they were said to number 500. The census of 1910 returned 82.

Connection in which they have become noted.—Palouse or Pelouse River, in Idaho and Washington, and the city of Palouse in Whitman County, Washington, preserve the name of the Palouse Indians.

Pshwanwapam. Meaning "the stony ground." Also called Upper Yakima.

Connections.—The Pshwanwapam belonged to the Shahaptian division of the Shapwailutan linguistic family, and probably were most closely connected with the Yakima.

Location.—On the upper course of Yakima River.

Puyallup. From Pwiya'lap, the native name of Puyallup River.

Connections.—The Puyallup belonged to the Nisqually dialectic group of the Coastal division of the Salishan linguistic family.

Location.—At the mouth of Puyallup River and the neighboring coast, including Carr Inlet and the southern part of Vashon Island.

Subdivisions and Villages

Esha'ktlabsh, on Hylebos Waterway.

Kalka'lak, at the mouth of Wappato Creek.

Klbalt, at Glencove.

Puyallup or Spwiya'laphabsh, on Commencement Bay and Puyallup River as far up as the mouth of Clarks Creek, including the main settlement of the same name at the mouth of Puyallup River.

Sha'tckad, where Clay Creek empties into the Puyallup River.

Sko'tlbabsh, on Carr Inlet, including a Sko'tlbabsh settlement on Carr Inlet above the town of Minter.

Skwapa'bsh, on the south part of Vashon Island and the land west of the Narrows, including a town of the same name at the mouth of a stream at Gig Harbor.

Skwlo'tsid, at the head of Wollochet Bay.

Steilacoom, on Steilacoom Creek and the neighboring beach, the main village on the present site of Steilacoom.

Tsugwa'lethl, at Quartermaster Harbor.

Tule'lakle, at the head of Burley Lagoon, Carr Inlet.

Twa'debshab, at the mouth of a creek formerly entering Commencement Bay and now covered by Tacoma.

Population.—(See **Nisqually.**) The report of the United States Office of Indian Affairs for 1937 gave 322 Puyallup.

Connections in which they have become noted.—The name Puyallup is preserved by a river, an Indian reservation, a glacier, an important town in Pierce County, and in the ridge called Puyallup Cleaver.

Queets or Quaitso. Significance unknown.

Connections.—The Queets belonged to the Coastal division of the Salishan linguistic family and were most intimately related to their neighbors to the south, the Quinault.

Location.—On Queets River and its branches.

Population.—Lewis and Clark in 1805 estimated that the Queets numbered 250. They then occupied 18 houses. Mooney (1928) estimated that in 1780 they and the Quinault together numbered 1,500, but Olson (1936) regards this figure as too high. Olson prints an estimate of 82 as their present population, including 23 males over 18, 32 females over 14, and 16 children between 6 and 16. In 1909 there were 62.

Connection in which they have become noted.—The name of the Queets is perpetuated in that of Queets River.

Quileute. Meaning unknown.

Connections.—Together with the Hoh and Chimakum, the Quileute constituted the Chimakuan linguistic family which is possibly more remotely related to Wakashan and Salishan.

Location.—On Quilayute River, on the west coast of Washington. They are now on the Quileute and Makah Reservations.

Population (including the Hoh).—Mooney (1928) estimates that in 1780 there were of the Quileute and the Hoh 500 Indians. Olson (1936) quotes a figure of 64 in 1888. The census of 1910 returned 303 and the United States Office of Indian Affairs in 1937 gave 284.

Connections in which they have become noted.—The town of Quillayute in Clallam County, preserves the name of the Quileute and it was formerly that of Soleduck River. Otherwise the tribe is particularly noted on account of the uniqueness of its language, which was spoken by no other known tribes except the Hoh and Chimakum (q. v.).

Quinault. "A corruption of kwi'naił, the name of the largest settlement situated at the present site of the village (Taholah)" at the mouth of the Quinault River.

Connections.—The Quinault belonged to the coastal division of the Salishan linguistic family.

Location.—The valley of Quinault River and the Pacific coast between Raft River and Joe Creek.

Subdivisions

Lewis and Clark mention a division or associated band called Calasthocle.

Towns

(Olson's (1936) list modified phonetically)

A'alatsis, 3 miles below Lake Quinault.
Djagaka'lmik, ½ mile above Nosklako's.
Djekwe'ls, on the north bank of Quinault River about 400 yards above Thlathle'lap).
Gutse'lps, 6 miles below Lake Quinault.
Hagwi'shtap, about 1½ miles above Cook Creek.
He'shnithl or Kuku'mnithl, on the south bank of Quinault River about 500 yards above Pini'lks.
Kwakwa'h, not far from Hagwi'shtap.

Kwakwa'nikatctan, 4 miles below Lake Quinault.
Kwatai'tamik, 3 miles above Kwakwa'h.
Kwatai'tumik, on the south bank about 500 yards above Kwi'naithl.
Kwikwa'la, perhaps ½ mile above Sunuksunu'ham.
Kwi'naithl, at present site of Taholah.
Lae'lsnithl, on north bank a mile or less above Heshnithl.
La'lshithl, perhaps a mile above Djagaka'lmik on Quinault River.
Ma'atnithl, 1 mile below the fork of upper Quinault River.
Magwa'ksnithl, 300 yards above Kwikwa'la.
Me'tsugutsathlan, on south bank of Quinault River at its mouth.
Nago'olatcan, not far from Nossho'k.
Negwe'thlan, at the mouth of Cook Creek.
Nokedja'kt or Thla'a'lgwap, on south bank a few hundred yards above Tonans.
Nomi'lthlostan, just above Kwakwa'h.
No'omo'thlapsh, at mouth of Moclips River, which bears its name in a corrupted form.
No'omo'thlapshtcu, not far above Magwa'ksnithl.
No'skathlan, a few miles above Kwi'naithl, on the north bank of Quinault River.
Noskthlako's, on south bank of Quinault River perhaps 1 mile above No'skathlan.
Nossho'k, not far above Nokedja'kt.
No'sthluk, not far from Djekwe'ls.
Pina'alathl, located where the upper Quinault River enters Lake Quinault.
Pini'lks, close to La'lshithl.
Pino'otcan tci'ta, on the upper Quinault below Ma'anithl.
Po'iks, on the upper Quinault above Finley Creek.
Pote'lks, 1 mile above Tsimi'sh.
Sunuksunu'ham, not far from Nomi'lthlostan.
Tamo'ulgutan, just below No'omo'thlapshtcu.
Tci'tano'sklakalathl, at the outlet of Lake Quinault.
Thlathle'lap, at the mouth of Quinault River and on the north bank.
To'nans, less than ½ mile above He'shnithl.
Tsi'i'sh, 2 miles above Magwaksnithl.

Population.—Lewis and Clark in 1805 estimated 800 Quinault proper and 200 Calasthocle. Mooney (1928) estimated 1,500 in 1780 including the Quaitso, but Olson (1936) suggests 800 and regards that as too high if anything. This would reduce Mooney's figure considerably since the Quaitso were a much smaller tribe. A tabulation recovered by Olson but believed to be from some Indian agent gave 95 Quinault in 1888. The Indian Office figure for the two tribes in 1907 was 196. The census of 1910, however, returned 288, presumably including the Quaitso. In 1923 the Indian Office returned 719 on the Quinault Reservation, perhaps representing several tribes, but that for 1937 gave 1,228 of the Quinault alone.

Connection in which they have become noted.—Quinault Lake and River and a small town, all in Grays Harbor County, preserve the name of the Quinault.

Sahehwamish. Meaning unknown but evidently that of a locality.

Connections.—The Sahehwamish belonged to the Nisqually dialectic group of the coastal division of the Salishan linguistic stock.

Location.—On the innermost inlets of Puget Sound as indicated by the positions of the subdivisions given below.

Subdivisions

Elo'sedabsh, on Medicine Creek and the lower reaches of Nisqually River, including a main settlement at the mouth of Nisqually River and Tuda'dab, at the mouth of McAllister or Medicine Creek.

Sahehwamish or Sahe'wabsh, on Shelton Inlet, including the main settlement of Sahe'wabsh, at Arcadia, and a village opposite the town of Shelton.

Skwayaithlhabsh, on Mud Bay or Eld Inlet.

Statca'sabsh, on Budd Inlet, with its principal settlement at Tumwater.

Tapi'ksdabsh, with its main settlement on Oyster Bay or Totten Inlet below the town of Oyster Bay.

Tutse'tcakl, on South Bay or Henderson Inlet, between the creek at the head and that on the south.

Population.—The group to which this tribe belonged is estimated by Mooney (1928) to have numbered 1,200 in 1780, and he gives 780 for the year 1907.

Samish. Signification unknown.

Connections.—The Samish belonged to the coastal division of the Salishan linguistic family.

Location.—On Samish Bay and Samish Island, Guemes Island, and the northwest portion of Fidalgo Island. The Samish were later placed on Lummi Reservation.

Villages

Atse'ked, on the south side of the slough at Edison on Samish Bay.

Dikwi'bthl.

Gunguna'la, on Guemes Island facing west toward Cypress Island.

Hwaibathl, at Anacortes.

Kwalo'l, at Summit Park on Fidalgo Bay.

Nukhwhaiimikhl, on the southwest side of Guemes Island.

The name of the last village listed above is from Gibbs (1877) and may be another name for Gunguna'la, and Gibbs' Aseakum is perhaps Atse'ked.

Population.—Mooney (1928) estimates the Samish tribe, together with the Lummi and Nooksack, at 1,000 in 1780. No later estimate is given.

Connection in which they have become noted.—Samish River, Samish Bay, Samish Island, and a post hamlet on Bellingham Bay perpetuate the name of the Samish Indians.

Sanpoil. A native word in spite of its French aspect; meaning unknown. Also called:

Hai-ai'-nĭma, by the Yakima.

Ipoilq, another Yakima name.

Nesilextcĭ'n, .n.selixtcĭ'n, by Sanpoil, and probably meaning "Salish-speaking."

N'poch-le, a shortened form of the name.

Connections.—The Sanpoil belonged to the inland division of the Salishan linguistic stock, and were related most closely to its eastern section.

Location.—On Sanpoil River and Nespelem Creek and on the Columbia below Big Bend. They were later placed on Sanpoil and Colville Reservations.

Subdivisions and Villages

The Nespelim of Nespelem Creek were often given independent status. Ray gives the following villages and camps:

Nespelim villages:

- Haimisahun, a summer settlement of the Suspiluk, on the north bank of Columbia River about a half mile above the mouth of Nespelem River.
- Masmasalimk, home of the Smasmasalimkuwa, approximately a mile and a half above Skik.
- Nekuktshiptin, home of the Snekuktshiptimuk, at the site of the present Condon's Ferry, on the north side of the river.
- Nspilem, home of the Snspiluk, on the lower Nespelem from the falls to the mouth of the river.
- Salkuahuwithl, home of the Salkuahuwithlau, across the river from the present town of Barry.
- Skik, home of the Skik, about a mile above Salkuahuwithl on the same side of the river.
- Skthlamchin, fishing grounds of the Salkuahuwithlau, across the river from the mouth of the Grand Coulee.

Sanpoil villages:

- Enthlukaluk, about a mile and a half north of the mouth of the river.
- Hahsulauk, home of the Shahsulauhuwa, near Plum.
- Hulalst, home of the S-hulalstu, at Whitestone, about 8 miles above Npuiluk.
- Hwatsam, a winter camp, about 3 miles above Snukeilt.
- Kakamkam, on the islands in the Sanpoil River a short distance above the mouth.
- Kathlpuspusten, home of the Kathlpuspustenak, about a mile above Plum, on the opposite side of the river.
- Ketapkunulak, on the banks of the Columbia just east of the Sanpoil River.
- Naak, home of the Snaakau, about a mile below Plum but on the north side of the river.
- Nhohogus, fishing grounds of the S-hulalstu.
- Npokstian, a winter camp, about 2 miles above Hwatsam.
- Npuiluk, home of the Snpuiluk, at the mouth of Sanpoil River, made up of the following camps: Snkethlkukwiliskanan, near the present landing of the Keller ferry; a branch of the last called by the same name, several hundred yards north of the first between the cliff and the Sanpoil River, on the west side; Kethltselchin, on the first bench above the Columbia, west of the Sanpoil River.
- Nthlahoitk, a winter camp of the Snpuiluk, about halfway between Skthlamchin and Naak.
- Saamthlk, home of the Saamthlk, on the opposite side of the river from Kathlpuspusten.
- Skekwilk, on the west side of Sanpoil River about a mile above the mouth.

Snputlem, on the east bank of Sanpoil River, about an eighth of a mile above the mouth.

Snukeilt, home of the Snukeiltk, on the west side of Columbia River about ½ mile above the mouth of Spokane River.

Tkukualkuhun, home of the Stkukualkuhunak, at Rodger's Bar just across the river from Hunters.

Tsaktsikskin, a winter camp of the Snpuiluk, about a half mile below Naak.

Wathlwathlaskin, home of the Swathlwathlaskink, ½ mile up the river from Nthlahoitk.

Temporary camp sites of the Sanpoil on Sanpoil River; beginning with the first temporary camp beyond Npuiluk:

Enluhulak, about 3 miles above the mouth of the river.

Ksikest, on the west side of the river about halfway between the Columbia River and Keller.

Aklaiyuk, ½ mile above Ksikest.

Snkloapeten, a short distance below Keller.

Pupesten, at the present site of Keller.

Nmhoyam, about a quarter of a mile north of Keller.

Nhwiipam, a mile above Alice Creek on the east side of the river.

Seaachast, at Alice Creek.

Achhulikipastem, about half a mile north of Alice Creek.

Nloklokekuelikten, about 2 miles south of Cash Creek.

Nhatlchinitk, on the west side of the river at Cash Creek.

Snthulusten, on the east side of the river at the foot of a cliff, about ¼ mile above Cash Creek.

Nlupiam, 1½ miles above Snthulusten, on the same side of the river.

Slakumulemk, directly across the river from Nlupiam.

Nklakachin, on the east side of the river, at Thirty-mile Creek.

Malt, ½ mile above Thirty-mile Creek.

Lulukhum, at Devil's Elbow.

The following possible camp sites are higher up:

Akthlkapukwithlp, 8 miles below West Fork.

Kthliipus, at the present site of Republic.

Tkwiip, near the creek at West Fork.

Population.—Mooney (1928) estimates 800 Sanpoil in 1780 but Ray (1932) raises this to 1,600–1,700, and considers that there were about 1,300 immediately following the middle of the nineteenth century. In 1905 the United States Indian Office returned 324 Sanpoil and 41 Nespelim; in 1910 the census gave 240 and 46; in 1913, as the result of a survey, the Office of Indian Affairs returned 202 and 43.

Connection in which they have become noted.—Sanpoil River, a northern tributary of the Columbia, perpetuates the name of the Sanpoil. Nespelem River is named for the subgroup, and a town.

Satsop. Significance unknown.

Connections.—The Satsop belonged to the coastal division of the Salishan linguistic family, and have usually been classed with the Lower Chehalis.

Location.—On Satsop River, a branch of the Chehalis.

Population.—The population of the Satsop is usually given with that of the Chehalis (q. v.), but in 1888 a census of the Satsop alone, obtained by Olson (1936), gave 12.

Connections in which they have become noted.—Satsop River and a village called Satsop in Grays Harbor County preserve the name of the Satsop.

Semiahmoo. Significance unknown. Also called:

Birch Bay Indians, from a place occupied by them.

Connections.—The Semiahmoo belonged to the coastal division of the Salishan linguistic stock.

Location.—About Semiahmoo Bay in northwest Washington and southwest British Columbia.

Population.—In 1843 the Semiahmoo numbered 300; in 1909 there were 38 in British Columbia; none were enumerated on the American side of the line.

Connections in which they have become noted.—The name of the Semiahmoo is preserved in Semiahmoo Bay and a township in Whatcom County, Wash.

Senijextee. Significance unknown. Also called:

Lake Indians, a popular name for them because they lived on the Arrow Lakes.

Connections.—The Senijextee belonged to the inland division of the Salishan linguistic stock, and were most closely connected with the Sanpoil.

Location.—On both sides of the Columbia River from Kettle Falls to the Canadian boundary, the valley of Kettle River, Kootenay River from its mouth to the first falls, and the region of the Arrow Lakes, B. C. The Lake Indians on the American side were placed on Colville Reservation.

Population.—Mooney (1928) estimates their numbers at 500 in 1780. In 1909 the United States Office of Indian Affairs reported 342 on Colville Reservation. The census of 1910 identifies them with the Colville and returns 785.

Sinkaietk. Significance unknown; an Anglicized form of their own name.

Connections.—The Sinkaietk are sometimes classed with the Okanagon, and called Lower Okanagon, both constituting a dialectic group of interior Salishan Indians.

Location.—Okanagan River from its mouth nearly to the mouth of the Similkameen.

Subdivisions

Kartar, from the foot of Lake Omak to the Columbia River.

Konkonelp, winter sites, from about 3 miles above Malott to the turn of the Okanagan River at Omak.

Tonasket, from Riverside upstream to Tonasket.

Tukoratum, winter sites, from Condon's Ferry on the Columbia to the mouth of the Okanagan River and up the latter to about 4 miles above Monse, Wash. Ray (1932) mentions four villages belonging to the Kartar and Tukoratum Bands.

Population.—Included with the Okanagon (q. v.).

Sinkakaius. Meaning "between people."

Connections.—The Sinkakaius belonged to the interior division of the Salishan linguistic stock and were composed largely of people from the Tukoratum Band of Sinkaietk and the Moses Columbia people.

Location.—Between Columbia River and the Grand Coulee in the latitude of Waterville.

Skagit. Significance unknown. Also called:

Hum-a-luh, own name, meaning "the people."

Connections.—The Skagit belonged to the coastal division of the Salishan linguistic stock.

Location.—On Skagit and Stillaguamish Rivers except about their mouths.

Subdivisions and Villages

(Smith, 1941)

Base'lelotsed, on Skagit River from Van Horn to roughly 3 miles above Rockport and Sauk River almost to the mouth of Suiattle, including the village of Tca'gwalk, at the mouth of Sauk River.

Baska'dsadsiuk, on the south bank of Skagit River from Hamilton to Birdsview, including a village opposite Hamilton.

Baske'kwiuk, on Skagit River above Rockport, including a village at Marble Mount at the mouth of the Cascade River.

Baslo'halok, on the north bank of the Skagit from Hamilton to Birdsview, including a settlement at Hamilton.

Duwa'ha, on the mainland drainages from South Bellingham to Bayview including part of Lake Whatcom, Lake Samish and Samish River, including the village of Batsla'thllaos, at Bayview on Padilla Bay.

Nookachamps, on Skagit River from Mount Vernon to Sedro Woolley and Nookachamps River drainage including Big Lake, including a village back of Mount Vernon just below the concrete bridge, and Tsla'tlabsh on Big Lake.

Sauk, on Sauk River above the confluence of the Suiattle River, including a settlement on Sauk prairie above Darrington.

Sba'leuk, on Skagit River from above Birdsview to above Concrete, including a village at Concrete.

Sikwigwi'lts, on Skagit River from Sedro Woolley to below Lyman, including a village on the flats near Sedro Woolley.

Stillaguamish, on Stillaguamish River from Arlington up, including villages at Arlington and Trafton.
Suiattle, on Suiattle River, including a village not far about the mouth of Suiattle River.
Tcubaa'bish, on Skagit River from Lyman to below Hamilton, including Day Creek drainage, and including a village at the mouth of Dry Creek.

Population.—The Skagit population is given by Mooney (1928), with the Swinomish and some other tribes, as 1,200 in 1780. Gibbs (1877) estimated there were 300 Skagit proper in 1853. The census of 1910 returned 56 under this name. In 1923 the United States Indian Office entered 221 "Swinomish" in their returns, including evidently the Skagit and some other tribes; in 1937 it gave an estimate of 200 Skagit.

Connection in which they have become noted.—Skagit River, which flows into Puget Sound, Skagit County, and a post hamlet preserve the name of the Skagit Indians.

Skilloot. Significance unknown.

Connections.—The Skilloot belonged to the Clackamas dialectic division of the Chinookan linguistic family.

Location.—On both sides of Columbia River above and below the mouth of Cowlitz River. (See also Oregon.)

Subdivisions and Villages

Cooniac (at Oak Point on the south side of Columbia River, below the mouth of the Cowlitz, in the present Columbia County, Oregon) was their principal village in later times. The Hullooetell, reported to Lewis and Clark as a numerous nation north of Columbia River on Cowlitz and Lewis Rivers, may have been a subdivision, although perhaps Salishan. The Seamysty, at the mouth of Cowlitz River before 1835, were undoubtedly a Skilloot band, and the Thlakalama and Tlakatlala of Boas (1901, and personal information 1905), at the mouth of Kalama River, about 3 miles above Oak Point, had best be added.

Population.—Mooney (1928) estimates the number of Skilloot at 3,250 in 1780 including 250 Tlakalama. In 1806 Lewis and Clark give 2,500 and in 1850 Lane places the Skilloot population at 200. They have now entirely disappeared as an independent group.

Skin. Taken from a town name.

Connections.—The Skin belonged to the Shahaptian division of the Shapwailutan linguistic stock.

Location.—On Columbia River from The Dalles to a point about 75 miles above.

Villages

Ka'sawi, on the Columbia opposite the mouth of Umatilla River.
Skin, opposite the mouth of Deschutes River.
Uchi'chol, on the north bank of the Columbia in Klickitat County.
Waiya'mpam, about Celilo.

Eneeshur is used by Lewis and Clark for part of the above people, perhaps all of them.

Population.—Mooney (1928) includes the Skin in a group under the general name Tapanash, which he estimates to have numbered 2,200 in 1780.

Snohomish. Meaning unknown but evidently the name of a place. Also called:

Ashnuhumsh, Kalapuya name.

Connections.—The Snohomish belonged to the Nisqually dialectic group of the coastal division of the Salishan linguistic stock.

Location.—On the lower course of Snohomish River and on the southern end of Whidbey Island.

Subdivisions and Villages

Sdugwadskabsh, the south portion of Whidbey Island, including villages opposite Mukilteo on Whidbey (Neg^{u}ā'sx) Island and at Newell on Useless Bay.

Skwilsi'diabsh, from Preston Point, above Everett, to the southern tip of Camano Island, including a village at Marysville and Tcatcthlks opposite Tulalip on Tulalip Bay.

Snohomish, Port Gardner Bay and Snohomish River as far up as Snohomish, including Tctlaks at Everett on the south side of the mouth of Snohomish River and Hibolb on the north side of its mouth.

Tukwetlbabsh, on Snohomish River from Snohomish to Monroe, including villages at Snohomish at the mouth of Pilchuck Creek and below Monroe 2 miles from the confluence of the Skykomish and the Snoqualmie.

Population.—Mooney (1928) estimated the population of the Snohomish, the Snoqualmie, the Tulalip, and some others at 1,200 in 1780. In 1850 there were 350 Snohomish. The census of 1910 gives 664, evidently including other bands, and the United States Office of Indian Affairs, 667 in 1937.

Connections in which they have become noted.—The name of the Snohomish is perpetuated in Snohomish River, Snohomish County, and a city in that county.

Snoqualmie. From the native word sdo'kwalbiuq^u.

Connections.—The Snoqualmie belonged to the Nisqually branch of the coastal division of the Salishan linguistic family.

Location.—On Snoqualmie and Skykomish Rivers.

Subdivisions and Villages

Skykomish, on Skykomish River above Sultan, and on the same below Goldbar.

Snoqualmie, on Snoqualmie River, including villages at Cherry Valley, on Snoqualmie River opposite the mouth of Tolt River; at Fall City; and below Snoqualmie Falls.

Stakta'ledjabsh, on Skykomish River as far up as Sultan, including Sultan Creek, including villages above Monroe at the mouth of Sultan Creek and on Sultan Creek 4 miles above its mouth.

877646—52——29

Population.—(See **Snohomish.**) The population of the Snoqualmie alone was reported as 225 in 1857.

Connections in which they have become noted.—The name of the Snoqualmie is perpetuated by Snoqualmie River and a town upon it in King County.

Spokan. Phonetically Spōkē'.n or Spō.qē'in); said by some to signify "Sun (people)," though this origin is doubtful. Also called:

Lêclē'cuks, Wasco name probably intended for this tribe.
Lar-ti-e-lo, by Lewis and Clerk in 1806.
Senoxamī'naex, by the Okanagon, from their principal division.
Sentutū' or Senoxma'n, by the Upper Kutenai from the Salish names for the Middle and Little Spokan respectively.

Connections.—The Spokan belonged to the inland division of the Salishan linguistic stock, and were most closely connected with the Kalispel, Pend d'Oreilles, Sematuse, and Salish.

Location.—On the Spokane and Little Spokane Rivers, southward to, and perhaps including, Cow Creek, and northward to include all of the northern feeders of the Spokane. (See also Idaho and Montana.)

Subdivisions

The Lower Spokan (about the mouth and on the lower part of Spokane River, including the present Spokane Indian reserve), the Upper Spokan or Little Spokan (occupying the valley of the Little Spokane River and all the country east of the lower Spokane to within the borders of Idaho), the South or Middle Spokan (occupying at least the lower part of Hangmans Creek, extending south along the borders of the Skitswish).

History.—Like so many other tribes of the Columbia region, the Spokan enter the arena of history with the appearance of Lewis and Clark in their territory in 1805. Teit (1930) thinks it possible that the several bands were once so many distinct tribes which have become fused in course of time, but of this there is no certainty. The Lower and most of the Middle Spokan, and part of the Upper Spokan, were finally placed under the Colville Agency; the rest are on the Flathead Reservation in Montana.

Population.—Mooney (1928) estimated that about 1780 there might have been 1,400 Spokan, but Teit's figures would raise this to something like 2,500. In 1806 Lewis and Clark thought there were 600 but they may have included only one of the three divisions. In 1905 the United States Indian Office gave 277 Lower Spokan and 177 Middle and Upper Spokan under the Colville Agency and 135 on the Flathead Reservation; in 1909 it gave 509 all together under the Colville Agency and 138 on the Flathead Reservation. The United States Census of 1910 returned 643 all told; the Indian Office Report for 1923, 669; and the Indian Office Report for 1937, 847.

Connections in which they have become noted.—The fame of the Spokan will rest in the future mainly upon the importance of the Washington city of Spokane. Their name is also attached to a river in Idaho and Washington, and to the county of which Spokane is the metropolis. It has also been applied to post hamlets in Custer County, S. Dak.; in Christian County, Mo.; and in Trumbull County, Ohio; also to Spokane Bridge, Spokane County, Wash.

Squaxon or **Squakson.** Their own name.

Connections.—The Squaxon belonged to the Nisqually branch of the coast division of the Salishan linguistic family.

Location.—On North Bay, Puget Sound.

Villages

On North Bay at the mouth of Coulter Creek and at Allyn at the mouth of Mason Creek.

Population.—With the Skokomish and Toanho (Twana), Mooney (1928) estimated that there were 1,000 Squaxon in 1780. In 1909 there were 98 under this name, and in 1937, 32.

Suquamish. From a native place name.

Connections.—They belonged to the Nisqually branch of the coastal division of the Salishan linguistic stock, their closest connections being with the Duwamish. The famous Seattle was chief of both tribes.

Location.—On the west side of Puget Sound, according to Paige (1857) claiming the territory from Applegate Cove to Gig Harbor.

Subdivisions and Villages

Saktabsh, on Sinclair Inlet, Dyes Inlet, and southern Blakely, Blakely Island, with villages at Bremerton and on Eagle Harbor.

Suquamish, on Liberty Bay, at Port Madison, and on the northern part of Blakely Island, with villages at Suquamish, above Poulsbo, and at Point Monroe.

Population.—(See **Duwamish.**) The Suquamish numbered 441 in 1857, 180 in 1909, and 307 in 1910, according to the census of that year. The United States Indian Office returned 204 "Susquamish" Indians in 1910, probably meaning this tribe. In 1937 it returned 168 "Suquamish."

Connection in which they have become noted.—The name Suquamish is applied to a town in Kitsap County, Wash.

Swallah. A name applied by Eells (1889). Also called:

Swalash, by Mallet (*in* Ind. Aff. Rep., 1877, p. 198).

Connections.—The Swallah belonged to the coastal division of the Salishan linguistic family.

Location.—On Orcas Island and San Juan Island and the group to which they belong.

Villages

Hutta'tchl, on the southeast end of Orcas Island.
Klala'kamish, on the east side of San Juan Island.
Lemaltcha, on Waldron Island.
Stashum, on Waldron Island.

Swinomish. A place name.

Connections.—The Swinomish belonged to the coastal division of the Salishan linguistic family, and are sometimes called a subdivision of the Skagit.

Location.—On the northern part of Whidbey Island and about the mouth of Skagit River.

Subdivisions and Villages

Ho'baks, on the upper end of Penn's Cove, not far from San de Fuca, Batsa'dsali at Coupeville, Ba'asats between Coupeville and Snaklem Point west of Long Point, and Tcubaa'ltced on the north side of Snaklem Point about 4 miles from Coupeville.

Kikia'los, on Skagit Bay from the South Fork of Skagit River to the north tip of Camano Island, with a village at the mouth of Carpenter Creek between Conway and Fir, and another called Atsala'di at Utsalady on Camano Island.

Kwa'dsakbiuk, on the lower reaches of Stillaguamish River and Port Susan, with a village at the mouth of the Stillaguamish.

Skagit, on Whidbey Island, from Oak Harbor south to Snaklem Point, with a village at Oak Harbor.

Skwada'bsh, on the North Fork of the Skagit River and the eastern part of Whidbey Island lying north of Oak Harbor, with Skwi'kwikwab at the mouth of the North Fork of the Skagit, and Tcotab on a point across Skagit Bay.

Swinomish (on southern Padilla Bay, Swinomish Slough which joins Padilla Bay and Skagit Bay, Skagit Bay from Sullivan Slough north, and the southeast portion of Fidalgo Island), with the following villages: Kale'kut (not far from Whitney at the highway bridge), Sde'os (near Lone Tree Point, Shuptada'tci (on Swinomish Slough 3 miles from La Conner), and another village (on Sullivan Slough just east of La Conner).

Population.—The Swinomish are usually enumerated with the Skagit (q. v.). The Skagit and Swinomish together numbered 268 in 1909. In 1937 there were 285 Swinomish reported.

Taidnapam. Also called Upper Cowlitz.

Connections.—The Taidnapam belonged to the Shahaptian division of the Shapwailutan linguistic family.

Location.—On the headwaters of Cowlitz River and perhaps extending over into the headwaters of the Lewis River.

Population.—Mooney estimates the population of the Taidnapam and the Klickitat together at 600 in 1780, but extinct as independent tribes by 1907.

Twana. Said to signify "a portage," referring to that between the upper end of Hoods Canal and the headwaters of Puget Sound. Also called:

Tu-a'd-hu, own name.
Skokomish, from the name of a principal division.
Wi'lfa Ampa'fa ami'm, Luckiamute-Kalapuya name.

Connections.—The Twana constituted one dialectic group of the coastal division of the Salishan stock.

Location.—On both sides of Hoods Canal. Later they were placed on Skokomish Reservation.

Subdivisions and Villages

Eels (1877) gave the following:

Kolsid, on Quilcene and Dabop Bays.
Skokomish, around Annas Bay and the drainage area of Skokomish River.
Soatlkobsh, on both sides of the canal from Seabeck and Oak Head to Port Gamble and Squamish Harbor opposite.

Smith (1941) lists the following villages:

Habha'b, at Eldon on the Canal at the mouth of the Hammerhammer River.
Li'liwap, at Lilliwap on the Canal.
Skoko'bsh, at the mouth of the Skokomish River.
Tule'lalap, at the east branch of the Canal at the mouth of Mission Creek.
Two towns at Duckabush and Brinnon.

Population.—Mooney (1928) gives the Twana, Skokomish, and Squaxon together a population of 1,000 in 1780. In 1853 they were estimated to total about 265. The census of 1910 gave 61 Twana and 195 Skokomish, and the United States Office of Indian Affairs returned 206 Skokomish in 1937.

Wallawalla. Meaning "little river"; called Walula by Spier (1936).

Connections.—The Wallawalla language belongs to the Shahaptian division of the Shapwailutan linguistic stock and is very closely related to the Nez Percé.

Location.—On the lower Wallawalla River, except perhaps for an area around Whitman occupied by Cayuse, and a short span along the Columbia and Snake Rivers near their junction, in Washington and Oregon. They are now on Umatilla Reservation, Oregon.

Population.—Mooney (1928) gives 1,500 for the Wallawalla and the Umatilla together in 1780. In 1805 Lewis and Clark estimated 1,600 but they included other bands now known to be independent. The census of 1910 gave 397, the Report of the United States Office of Indian Affairs for 1923, 628, and that for 1937, 631, the two last evidently including some other peoples.

Connections in which they have become noted.—The name Wallawalla is perpetuated in that of the city of Walla Walla, Wash.; Walla Walla County; Walla Walla River, which flows through Oregon and Washington; and appears in the name of a small place in Illinois.

Wanapam. Significance unknown.

Connections.—The Wanapam belonged to the Shahaptian division of the Shapwailutan linguistic stock and were connected closely with the Palouse.

Location.—In the bend of Columbia River between Priest Rapids and a point some distance below the mouth of Umatilla River, and extending east of the Columbia north of Pasco.

Subdivisions

They seem to have included two branches, the Chamnapum and Wanapam proper.

Population.—Mooney (1928) estimates their population as 1,800 in 1780.

Watlala. The Watlala occupied the north side of Columbia River from the Cascades to Skamania and perhaps to Cape Horn, but a larger territory on the south side. (See under Oregon.)

Wauyukma. Significance unknown.

Connections.—They belonged to the Shahaptian division of the Shapwailutan linguistic family and were very closely related to the Palouse.

Location.—On Snake River below the mouth of the Palouse.

Population.—Unknown but probably included with the Palouse, which Mooney (1928) estimates to have numbered 1,800 in 1780.

Wenatchee (Wīna'tc̣a). So called by the Wasco, and it has become a popular name for them. Also called:

Awena'tchela, by the Klickitat, meaning "people at the coming-out or source," said to refer to the fact that they occupied the country at the heads of the rivers or above the Yakima.

Pisquow, from .s.npeskwau'zux, their own name, variants of which appear in the appelations given them by other Salish tribes in the neighborhood.

Tsō'kwob.c, by the Snohomish.

Connections.—The Wenatchee belonged to the inland division of the Salishan linguistic family, their nearest relations being the Sinkiuse-Columbia Indians.

Subdivisions

(From Curtis (1907–9) and Ray (1932))

Sinia'lkumuk, on the Columbia between Entiat Creek and Wenatchee River.

Sinkumchi'muk, at the mouth of the Wenatchee.

Sinpusko'isok, at the forks of the Wenatchee, where the town of Leavenworth now stands.

Sintia'tkumuk, along Entiat Creek.
Stske'tamihu, 6 miles down river from the present town of Wenatchee.

Minor divisions mentioned are the following:

Camiltpaw, on the east side of Columbia River.
Shanwappom, on the headwaters of Cataract (Klickitat) and Tapteel Rivers.
Siapkat, at a place of this name on the east bank of Columbia River, about Bishop Rock and Milk Creek, below Wenatchee River.
Skaddal, originally on Cataract (Klickitat) River, on the west bank of Yakima River and later opposite the entrance to Selah Creek.

Location.—On Methow and Wenatchee Rivers and Chelan Lake. The Wenatchee are now under the Colville Agency.

Population.—Mooney (1928) estimated there were 1,400 Wenatchee in 1780, but Teit (1928) considers this considerably too low. The four bands of this tribe mentioned by Lewis and Clark in 1805 totaled 820. The census of 1910 gave 52.

Connection in which they have become noted.—Wenatchee River, Lake Wenatchee, and Wenatchee Mountain preserve the name, as also the town of Wenatchee, county seat of Chelan County.

Wishram. From Wu'cxam, the name given them by the Yakima and Klickitat Indians. Also called:

E-che-loot, by Lewis and Clark in 1806, from their own name.
Ila'xluit, their own name and from this called Tlakluit.

Connections.—They belonged to the Chinookan stock, and spoke the same dialect as the Wasco.

Location.—On the north side of Columbia River in Klickitat County.

Villages

Atatathlia itcagitkok, on a small island near Celilo Falls, or more likely Ten-Mile Rapids.
Chalaitgelit, a short distance east of The Dalles.
Gawilapchk, a winter village below The Dalles.
Gawishila, a fishing station above The Dalles.
Hladakhat, about 10 miles below The Dalles.
Hliluseltshlikh, below Big Eddy.
Kwalasints, opposite The Dalles.
Nayakkhachikh, a winter village below Gawilapchk.
Niukhtash, at Big Eddy.
Shabanahksh, 1 mile below Wishram (?).
Shgwaliksh, perhaps Klickitat, about 12 miles (?) below The Dalles.
Shikeldaptikh, about a half mile below The Dalles.
Shkagech, below Crate's Point.
Shkonana, opposite Crate's Point.
Shkukskhat, below The Dalles.
Tsapkhadidlit, a wintering place below Nayakkhachikh.
Waginkhak, below The Dalles and the lowest Tlakluit town on the river.
Wakemap, above Wishram.
Wasnaniks, below Skukskhat.
Wayagwa, above The Dalles, the easternmost town.
Wishram (properly called Nixlúidix'), about 5 miles above The Dalles.

Population.—Mooney (1928) estimated that in 1780 there were about 1,500 Wishram, but Spier and Sapir (1930) suggest 1,000 about 1800. The latter figure is the one given by Lewis and Clark in 1806. The census of 1910 returned 274, and in 1937, under the designation "Upper Chinook," the United States Office of Indian Affairs gave 124.

Connection in which they have become noted.—A town in Klickitat County preserves the name of the Wishram.

Wynoochee. Significance of word is unreported.

Connections.—The Wynoochee were closely connected with the Chehalis Indians and belonged to the coastal division of the Salishan linguistic stock.

Location.—On the Wynoochee, an affluent of Chehalis River.

Yakima. Meaning "runaway." Also called:

Cuts-sáh-nem, by Clark in 1805 in Lewis and Clark Journals (1904–5).
Pa' kiut'lĕma, own name, "people of the gap."
Shanwappoms, from Lewis and Clark in 1805.
Stobshaddat, by the Puget Sound tribes, meaning "robbers."
Waptai'lmĭn, own name, "people of the narrow river." Both of their names for themselves refer to the narrows in Yakima River at Union Gap where their chief village was formerly situated.

Connections.—The Yakima belonged to the Shahaptian division of the Shapwailutan linguistic family.

Location.—On the lower course of Yakima River.

Subdivisions

(As given by Spier (1936), quoting Mooney and Curtis)

Ătanum-lema, on Atanum Creek.
Nakchi'sh-hlama, on Naches River, and hence possibly Pshwa'nwapam.
Pisko, about the mouth of Toppenish Creek.
Se'tas-lema, on Satus Creek.
Si'-hlama, on Yakima River above the mouth of Toppenish Creek.
Si'la-hlama, on Yakima River between Wenas and Umtanum Creeks.
Si'mkoe-hlama, on Simcoe Creek.
Tkai'waichash-hlama, on Cowiche Creek.
Topinish, on Toppenish Creek.
Waptailmin, at or below Union Gap.

It is quite possible that under the term Yakima several distinct tribes were included.

History and location.—The Yakima are mentioned by Lewis and Clark under the name of Cutsahnim, but it is not known how many and what bands were included under that term. In 1855 the United States made a treaty with the Yakima and 13 other tribes of Shapwailutan, Salishan, and Chinookan stocks, by which these Indians ceded the territory from the Cascade Mountains to Palouse and Snake Rivers and from Lake Chelan to the Columbia. The Yakima

Reservation was established at the same time and upon it all the participating tribes and bands were to be confederated as the Yakima Nation under the leadership of Kamaiakan, a distinguished Yakima chief. Before this treaty could be ratified, however, the Yakima War broke out, and it was not until 1859 that its provisions were carried into effect. The Palouse and certain other tribes have never recognized the treaty or come on the reservation. Since the establishment of the reservation, the term Yakima has been generally used in a comprehensive sense to include all the tribes within its limits, so that it is now impossible to estimate the number of true Yakima.

Population.—Mooney (1928) estimated the Yakima proper at 3,000 in 1780. In 1806 Lewis and Clark give an estimated population of 1,200 to their Cutsahnim (see above). The census of 1910 gives 1,362 "Yakima," and the Report of the United States Indian Office for 1923, 2,939, but as already stated, this name now covers many people beside the true Yakima tribe. In 1937 the population of the same body of Indians was given as 2,933.

Connections in which they have become noted.—The Yakima first attained prominence on account of the extension of their name over a number of related, and some unrelated, peoples as above mentioned, and its use to designate the Yakima Reservation. It has attained greater permanence as the designation of a branch of Columbia River, a county in Washington, and a town in the same County and State.

OREGON

The history of the Oregon Indians was similar to that of the Indians of Washington. The coast tribes seem to have been affected little or not at all by the settlements of the Spaniards in California, and those of the interior were influenced only in slightly greater measure by them through the introduction of the horse. Nor were these tribes reached so extensively by the employees of the great fur companies. Contact with such advance agents of civilization was principally along the valley of the Columbia River, and Astoria will always be remembered as bearing witness to the transient attempts of the American Fur Company to establish a permanent trading organization in this region under the American flag. As in the case of Washington, Oregon and its tribes were first brought to the acquaintance of our Eastern States in an intimate way by the expedition of Lewis and Clark in 1805–6. Here also settlement was delayed until the fixation of the International Boundary line and the rush westward following upon the discovery of gold in California. From the middle of the nineteenth century onward, however, the native tribes were rapidly dispossessed, placed upon reservations, and reduced in numbers. At a later period the decrease became less marked, but it has continued nevertheless, partly as an actual extinction of the aboriginal population and partly as an absorption in the dominant race. Most of the Chinookan tribes were finally placed upon Warm Springs and Grande Ronde Reservations and on Yakima Reservation in Washington; all of the Athapascan tribes upon the Siletz Reservation, except the Umpqua, who went to Grande Ronde; the Kusan and Yakonan tribes upon the Siletz Reservation; the Salishan peoples of Oregon upon the Grande Ronde and Siletz Reserves; most of the Kalapooian peoples upon the Grande Ronde, though a few on the Siletz; most of the Molala upon the Grande Ronde; the Klamath upon Klamath Reserve; the Modoc mostly on Klamath Reserve but a few upon the Quapaw Reservation in Oklahoma; the Shahaptian tribes of Oregon upon the Umatilla Reservation; and the Northern Paiutes upon the Klamath Reservation.

Ahantchuyuk. Own name, significance unknown. Also called:

French Prairie Indians, by early settlers.
Pudding River Indians, by various authors, and adopted by Berreman (1937).

Connections.—The Ahantchuyuk belonged to the Kalapooian linguistic stock.

Location.—On and about Pudding River, which empties into the Willamette from the east about 10 miles south of Oregon City.

Population.—(See **Calapooya**.) Not given separately.

Alsea. A corruption of Älsé, their own name, meaning unknown. Also called:

Kûnis'tûnnĕ, Chastacosta name.
Päifan amím, Luckiamute Kalapuya name.
Si ni'-tĕ-lĭ tunnĕ, Naltunne name, meaning "flatheads."
Tcha yáχo amim, Luckiamute Kalapuya name.
Tĕhayesátlu, Nestucca name.

Connections.—The Alsea belonged to the Yakonan linguistic stock.

Location.—On Alsea River and Bay.

Villages

Chiink, on the south side of Alsea River.
Kakhtshanwaish, on the north side of Alsea River.
Kalbusht, on the lower course of Alsea River.
Kauhuk, on the south side of Alsea River.
Kaukhwan, on the north side of Alsea River at Beaver Creek.
Khlimkwaish, on the south side of Alsea River.
Khlokhwaiyutslu, on the north side of Alsea River.
Kutauwa, on the north side of Alsea River at its mouth.
Kwamk, on the south side of Alsea River.
Kwulisit, on the south side of Alsea River.

Kyamaisu, on the north side of Alsea River at its mouth.
Panit, on the south side of Alsea River.
Shiuwauk, on the north side of Alsea River.
Skhakhwaiyutslu, on the south side of Alsea River.
Tachuwit, on the north side of Alsea River.
Thlekuhweyuk, on the south side of Alsea River.
Thlekushauk, on the south side of Alsea River.

Population.—Mooney (1928) estimates the number of Indians belonging to the Yakonan stock at 6,000 in 1780. The census of 1910 returned 29 Indians under this name, and that of 1930 only 9 under the entire Yakonan stock.

Connection in which they have become noted.—Alsea or Alseya River, Alsea Bay and the village of Alsea, Benton County, Oreg., preserve the name of the Alsea Indians.

Atfalati. Meaning unknown. Often shortened to Fallatahs. Sometimes spelled Tuálati, or Tualatin (Berreman, 1937). Also known as:

Tualatin, Palmer *in* Ind. Aff. Rep., p. 260, 1859.
Wapato Lake Indians, a common name used by travelers.

Connections.—The Atfalati belonged to the northern dialectic branch of the Kalapooian linguistic family.

Location.—On the Atfalati plains, the hills about Forest Grove and the shores and vicinity of Wapato; they are also said to have extended as far as the site of Portland.

Villages and Bands

Chachambitmanchal, 3½ miles north of Forest Grove.
Chachamewa, at Forest Grove, 6 miles from Wapato Lake.
Chachanim, on Wapato Lake prairie.
Chachif, on Wapato Lake.
Chachimahiyuk, between Wapato Lake and Willamette River, Washington County.
Chachimewa, on or near Wapato Lake, Yamhill County.
Chachokwith, at a place of the same name north of Forest Grove, Washington County.
Chaginduefte i, between Hillsboro and Sauvies Island, Washington County.
Chahelim, in Chehelim Valley, 5 miles south of Wapato Lake, Yamhill County.
Chakeipi, about 10 miles west of Oregon City.
Chakutpaliu, northeast of Hillsboro, Washington County.
Chalal, near the outlet of Wapato Lake.
Chalawai, southeast of Wapato Lake.
Chamampit, on Wapato Creek at the east end of Wapato Lake.
Chapanaghtin, north of Hillsboro, Washington County.
Chapokele, 4 miles west of Wapato Lake.
Chapungathpi, at Forest Grove, Washington County.
Chatagihl, at the upper end of Wapato Lake.
Chatagithl, at the upper end of Wapato Lake.
Chatagshish, in Washington County.
Chatakuin, 7 miles north of Hillsboro, Washington County.

Chatamnei, 10 miles north of Wapato Lake, in Washington County.
Chatilkuei, 5 miles west of Wapato Lake, in Yamhill County.
Chawayed, west of Forest Grove, in Washington County.

Population.—(See **Calapooya.**) The census of 1910 returned 44 Atfalati.

Connection in which they have become noted.—The name Atfalati is preserved in the form Tualatin by a town in Washington County.

Bannock. The Bannock came over into the eastern borders of the state between Powder and Owyhee Rivers in more recent times. (See Idaho.)

Calapooya. Meaning unknown. Also called:

Kait-ka, by the Umpqua.
Tsänh-alokual amím, by the Luckiamute Kalapuya.

Connections.—The Calapooya belonged to the Calapooya dialectic division of the Kalapooian linguistic stock.

Location.—On the headwaters of Willamette River including McKinzie, Middle, and West Forks.

Subdivisions or Bands

Ampishtna, east of upper Willamette River.
Tsanchifin, on the site of Eugene City.
Tsanklightemifa, at Eugene City.
Tsankupi, at Brownsville, Lynn County.
Tsawokot, north of Eugene City.

Population.—Mooney (1928) estimates the population of the entire Kalapooian stock at 3,000 in 1780. The Kalapooian bands on Grande Ronde Reservation numbered 351 in 1880; 164 in 1890; 130 in 1905. The census of 1910 returned 5 of the Calapooya tribe by itself, and 106 in the entire stock; and that of 1930, 45 individuals in the stock.

Connections in which they have become noted.—The Calapooya tribe is of note (1) because its name has been used for all the tribes of the stock; and (2) from its later application to Calapooya River, a branch of the Willamette; Calapooya Creek, an affluent of the Umpqua; and the Calapooya Mountains.

Cayuse. Significance unknown.

Haí'luntchi, Molalla name.
Wailĕtpu, own name.

Connections.—The Cayuse were placed by Powell (1891) in the Waiilatpuan linguistic stock along with the Molala (q. v.), but this is now recognized as a branch of the Shapwailutan family.

Location.—About the heads of Wallawalla, Umatilla, and Grande Ronde Rivers and extending from the Blue Mountains to Deschutes River, Washington and Oregon.

History.—Anciently the Cayuse are said to have had their headquarters on the Upper Grande Ronde but to have extended west later to the region of Deschutes River, where they may have met the Molala. They entered the historical arena with the expedition of Lewis and Clark and were afterward well known to explorers, hunters, and settlers. In 1838 a mission was established among them by the noted Marcus Whitman at the site of the present town of Whitman, but in 1847 smallpox carried off a large number of the tribe, and the Indians, believing the missionaries to be the cause, murdered Whitman and a number of other Whites and destroyed the mission. By 1851 they were much reduced in numbers and had become partially merged in the Nez Percé. In 1853 they joined in the treaty by which Umatilla Reservation was formed and made their homes upon it from that time forward. Their language is now nearly extinct.

Population.—Mooney (1928) estimates 500 Cayuse in 1780. In 1904, 404 were officially reported; the census of 1910 gave 298, while the United States Indian Office in 1923 returned 337. The census of 1930 reported 199 Cayuse and Molala, and the United States Indian Office of Cayuse alone in 1937, 370.

Connection in which they have become noted.—The Cayuse were reputed one of the most warlike tribes of Washington and Oregon. Horses were early bred among them and an Indian pony came to be known to the white settlers as a "cayuse." There is a place called Cayuse in Umatilla County, Oreg.

Chastacosta. From Shista-kwŭsta, their own name, significance unknown. Also called:

Atcháshti amē'nmei, by the Atfalati Kalapuya.
Atchashti ámim, another form of the Kalapuya name.
Katuku, by the Shasta.
Wálamskni, by the Klamath.
Wálamswash, by the Modoc.

Connections.—The Chastacosta belonged to the Athapascan stock.

Location.—On the lower course of Illinois River, both sides of Rogue River for some distance above its confluence with the Illinois, and on the north bank somewhat farther.

Villages

Dorsey recorded the following:

Chetuttunne.
Chunarghuttunne, east of the junction of Rogue River and Applegate River.
Chunsetunneta.
Chunsetunnetun.
Chushtarghasuttun.
Chusterghutmunnetun, the highest on Rogue River.
Chuttushshunche.
Khloshlekhwuche.
Khotltacheche.
Khtalutlitunne.
Kthelutlitunne, at the junction of Rogue River and a southern affluent.
Kushlatata.
Mekichuntun.

Musme.
Natkhwunche.
Nishtuwekulsushtun.
Sechukhtun.
Senestun.
Setaaye.
Setsurgheake.
Silkhkemechetatun.
Sinarghutlitun.
Skurgnut.
Sukechunetunne.
Surghustesthitun.
Tachikhwutme, above the mouth of Illinois River.
Takasichekhwut.
Talsunme.
Tatsunye.
Thethlkhuttunne.
Tisattunne.
Tsetaame, east of the junction of Rogue River with Applegate River.
Tsetutkhlalenitun.
Tukulittatun.
Tukwilisitunne.
Tuslatunne.

Twenty of these at least were on the north side of Rogue River. The following may be synonymous with some in the above list: Klothchetunne, on or in the vicinity of Rogue River; Sekhatsatunne, on the north bank of Rogue River; Tasunmatunne, in the Rogue River country.

Drucker (1937) merely gives the "Chasta Costa (cista kwusta)" as one town near the Rogue-Illinois confluence divided into three parts called Tleattlī'ntun, Tcetcī'-wut, and Setla'tun.

Population.—Mooney (1928) estimates the population of the Chastacosta and 10 other Athapascan tribes in the vicinity at 5,600. In 1856 the remnant which was removed to Siletz Reservation numbered but 153, and the census of 1910 returned only 7. The 1930 census returned a total Athapascan population in Oregon of 504. The United States Office of Indian Affairs reported 30 Chastacosta in 1937.

Chelamela. Significance unknown. Also called:

Long Tom Creek Indians.

Connections.—The Chelamela belonged to the Calapooya dialectic division of the Kalapooian linguistic stock.

Location.—On Long Tom Creek, a western tributary of the Willamette River.

Population.—(See **Calapooya.**)

Chepenafa. Significance unknown. Also called:

Api'nefu, or Pineifu, by the other Kalapuya.
Marys River Indians, the official and popular name.

Connections.—The Chepenafa belonged to the Calapooya dialectic division of the Kalapooian linguistic stock, and were sometimes regarded as a subdivision of the Luckamiut (q. v.).

Location.—At the forks of St. Marys Creek, near Corvallis.

Population.—(See **Calapooya.**) The census of 1910 returned 24.

Chetco. Own name, meaning "close to the mouth of the stream."

Connections.—The Chetco belonged to the Athapascan linguistic stock and differed little in culture from the other Athapascan groups immediately north of them and the Tolowa to the south.

Location.—On each side of the mouth of Chetco River and about 14 miles up it as well as on Winchuck River. (See also California.)

Villages

As recorded by Dorsey (*in* Hodge, 1907):

Chettanne, Khuniliikhwut, Nukhsuchutun, Setthatun, Siskhaslitun, and Tachukhaslitun, on the south side of Chetco River.

Chettannene, on the north side of Chetco River.

Nakwutthume, on Chetco River above all the other villages.

Thlcharghiliitun, on the upper course of a south branch of Chetco River.

As recorded by Drucker (1937):

Hosa'tun, at the mouth of Winchuck River.

Natltene'tun, about where the modern town of Brookings stands.

Shrī'choslintun, on Chetco River a little above the following.

Tcagitlī'tun, on Chetco River at the mouth of the north Fork.

Tcet or Tcetko, at the mouth of Chetco River, really a town on each side.

Tūme'stun, near Shrī'choslintun.

Drucker adds that "the coast town which Parrish calls Wishtenatan (Waterman, xustene'ten) may have been affiliated more closely with Chetco River than with the Lower Rogue River group."

Population.—See Chastacosta. In 1854, a year after the Chetco had been removed to the Siletz Reservation, they numbered 241. In 1861 they numbered 262. In 1877 there were only 63 on the reservation. The census of 1910 returned 9.

Connection in which they have become noted.—A river and a post hamlet in Curry County, Oregon, perpetuate the name of the Chetco.

Clackamas. From their own name, Guithla'kimas, significance unknown.

Also spelled Tlăkĭmĭsh, and called:

A'kimmash, by the Atfalati Kalapuya.

Gitā'q!ēmas, by the Clatsop.

Nsekau's or Ns tiwat, by the Nestucca.

Tu'hu tane, by the Umpqua.

Connections.—The Clackamas belonged to the Chinookan linguistic stock and to a dialectical division to which they have given their name.

Location.—On Clackamas River, claiming the country on the east side of Willamette River from a few miles above its mouth nearly to Oregon City and east as far as the Cascade Mountains. (See also Washington.)

Population.—Mooney (1928) estimates that the Clackamas numbered 2,500 in 1780. In 1806 Lewis and Clark set down their probable number as 1,800. In 1851 there were 88; the 1910 census returned 40; and United States Office of Indian Affairs in 1937, 81. The census of 1930 reported a total of 561 Indians in the Chinookan stock.

Connection in which they have become noted.—The name Clackamas is perpetuated by a river, a county, and a town in Oregon.

Clatskanie. Significance unknown. Also spelled A'látskné-i, Clackstar, Klatskanai, Tlatskanai, etc.

Connection.—The Clatskanie belonged to the Athapascan linguistic stock.

Location.—According to Gibbs (1877) the Clatskanie at one time owned the prairies bordering Chehalis River, Washington, at the mouth of Skookumchuck River, but on the failure of game, crossed the Columbia and occupied the mountains about Clatskanie River, their best-known historic seat. For a long time they exacted toll of all who passed going up or down the Columbia.

Population.—Mooney (1928) estimates 1,600 Clatskanie in 1780. In 1851 they were reduced to three men and five women. The census of 1910 returned three. (See **Chastacosta.**)

Connection in which they have become noted.—Like the Kwahlioqua, the Clatskanie are noted for their isolation from other branches of the Athapascan stock. Their name is preserved by Clatskanie Creek and Clatskanie town in Columbia County, Oreg.

Clatsop. From a native word meaning "dried salmon."

Connection.—The Clatsop belonged to the Lower Chinook dialectic division of the Chinookan linguistic stock.

Location.—The Clatsop centered about Cape Adams, on the south side of Columbia River, extending up the latter as far as Tongue Point, and southward on the Pacific coast to Tillamook Head.

Villages

As far as known these were:

Konope, near the mouth of Columbia River.

Neacoxy, the principal winter village, at the site of Seaside, at the mouth of Neacoxie Creek.

Neahkeluk, at Point Adams.

Niakewankih, south of Point Adams at the mouth of Ohanna Creek.

Neahkstowt, near the present Hammond.

Necotat, at the site of Seaside.

Population.—Mooney (1928) estimates 300 Clatsop in 1780. In 1806 Lewis and Clark gave 300. In 1875 the few survivors were moved to Grande Ronde Reservation, where the census of 1910 returned 26. (See **Clackamas.**)

Connection in which they have become noted.—Clatsop County and the town of Clatsop, Oreg., preserve the name.

Clowwewalla. Significance unknown. Phonetically GiLā'wēwalamt. Also called:

Fall Indians, Tumwater Indians, popular names.

Willamette Indians, Willamette Falls Indians, popular names.

Connections.—The Clowwewalla belonged to the Clackamas division of the Chinookan linguistic stock.

Location.—At the falls of Willamette River.

Subdivisions

The Clowwewalla may have included the Cushooks, Chahcowahs, and Nemalquinner of Lewis and Clark.

Population.—The Clowwewalla, or a part of them, were called Cushook by Lewis and Clark, who estimated that they numbered 650 in 1805–6. On this basis Mooney (1928) estimated there might have been 900 in 1780. They were greatly reduced by the epidemic of 1829 and in 1851 numbered 13. They are now apparently extinct.

Dakubetede. Own name, significance unknown. Also called:

Applegate River Indians, from their habitat.
Nĭ'ckitc hĭtclûm, Alsea name, meaning "people far up the stream."
Ts'û-qûs-li'-qwŭt-me' tunne, Naltûnnetûnne name.

Connections.—The Dakubetede belonged to the Athapascan linguistic stock, using a dialect identical with that of the Taltushtuntude.

Location.—On Applegate River.

Population.—Mooney (1928) estimates the Dakubetede, the Nahankhotane (part of the Umpqua), the Taltushtuntude, and the Umpqua to have numbered 3,200 in 1780. They are nowhere separately enumerated. (See **Chastacosta.**)

Hanis. Own name, significance unknown.

Connections.—The Hanis formed one dialectic group of the Kusan linguistic family, the other being Miluk. It is probable that this stock was connected with the Yakonan.

Location.—On Coos River and Bay.

Villages

Anasitoh, on the south side of Coos Bay.
Melukitz, on the north side of Coos Bay.

Population.—Mooney (1928) estimates that the Hanis and the Miluk together numbered 2,000 in 1780. In 1805 Lewis and Clark estimated 1,500 Hanis. The census of 1910 returned 93 for the entire stock and that of 1930, 107, while, again for the stock, the United States Office of Indian Affairs reported 55 in 1937.

Klamath. A word of uncertain origin but probably used first by Columbia River or other outside tribes. Their own name is mâklaks, meaning "people," "community." They are also called:

Aígspaluma, abbreviated to Aígspalo, Aíspalu; Nez Percé name for all Indians on Klamath Reservation and in the vicinity, meaning "people of the chipmunks."

Alámmimakt ísh (from ala'mmig, "Upper Klamath Lake"), said to be the Achomawi name.
Athlámeth, Calapooya name.
Aúksiwash, in Yreka dialect of Shasta.
Dak'-ts!aᵃm-al-aᶜ or Dak'-ts!aᵉw-an-a'ᶜ, "those above the lakes," by the Takelma.
Ê-ukshik-ni máklaks, meaning "people of the lakes," also their own name.
Makaítserk, by the western Shasta.
Plaíkni, collective name for Klamath, Modoc, and Snakes on Sprague River.
Sáyi, Northern Paiute name.
Tapáadji, Ilmawi name.
Wols, name given by the Latgawa.

Connections.—Together with the Modoc (q. v.), the Klamath constituted the Lutuamian division of the Shapwailutan linguistic family.

Location.—On Upper Klamath Lake, Klamath Marsh, and Williamson and Sprague Rivers.

Subdivisions and Villages

These are given as follows by Spier (1930), maintaining his order:

I. ă'ukckni (the Klamath marsh—Williamson River group), with the following villages: mŭ'tcuia'ksi (near the bridge toward the eastern end of Klamath marsh), k'ᴇtaiwa's (along the eastern side of the marsh), gŭpgŭa'ḳsi, (east side of Klamath marsh south of last), i'wal (along a southeastern tongue of the marsh), kla'djŏḳsi (ibid.), du''ĭlḳŭt (on the south shore of Klamath marsh), awa'lwaskăn (west of preceding), wa'ktale's (on the higher ground where Williamson River leaves the marsh), la'laks (ibid.), lobŏ'kstsŏksi (on the bluff on the left bank of the Sprague River at the railroad bridge) called by Gatschet (1891 b) ktaí-tú-pakshi), an unnamed site (on the south side of Sprague River below the dam), ḳ!ŏtcwă'ĕts (about 2 miles above the dam on the south bank of Sprague River), komă'ĕksi (on both sides of Sprague River south of Braymill, 4 miles from Chiloquin), ḳa'umkăn (about 6 miles above last), [Yainax] (settlements of some sort near here), hĭcdĭc-luĕ'lukc (west of Gearhart Mountain), bᴇzŭkse'was (on the right bank of Williamson River below the mouth of Sprague River), tȧkalma'kcda (on the right bank of Williamson River below preceding), k'tai'di (on a flat opposite last mentioned), djĭgiă's (below last two on both sides of river), ḳ!o'ltawas (on both banks below preceding but principally on left bank), at'awĭkc (below last, principally on right bank), ya'ak (right bank below preceding), tsa'k'wi (below last, principally on right), wĭtă'mŭmpsi (on a high bluff on the right bank above an eddy in the sharp bend in the river), goyᴇmskė'ᴇgĭs or ki̇ᴇkė'tsŭs (on right bank below last), wᴇla'lksi (on the eastern shore of Agency Lake), loḳ'o'gŭt (on the higher land near Agency Lake by a little warm spring), tcŏ'klalŭmps (overlooks the lake where the Chiloquin road meets the Agency Lake highway), "other towns may have been at ya'mzi, on the western side of Yamsay Mountain, and kokėnă'oke, Spring Creek, a large northern affluent of Klamath marsh."

II. kowa'cdikni, perhaps part of the first division, occupying: kowa'cdi (on Agency Lake).

III. du'kwakni (on the delta of Williamson River), affiliated most closely with the next division, and including: mo'aḳsda (on the left bank of Williamson River nearly a mile above the mouth), wĭckămdi (below the preceding on the right bank), la'wa'lstŏt (on the point forming the right side of the mouth of Williamson River), mo'giŋkŭnks (on the left bank of Williamson River a quarter of a mile above the mouth), djĭŋgŭs (at a spring on the lake front to the east of the mouth of Williamson River).

IV. gu'mbŏtkni (on Pelican Bay and the marsh to the north) including: sle'tsksi (on the west side of Seven Mile Creek near its mouth), wudŏ'kăn (in the marsh a mile from the last and east of Seven Mile Creek), iwŭnau'ts (on the western side of a little creek emptying into Klamath Lake 2 miles east of Recreation P. O., and extending along the marsh shore to the northern side of Pelican Bay), dŭnŏ'ksi (an open space overlooking the northern end of Pelican Bay), e'o'ḳai (a few hundred yards up Four Mile Creek on the left bank), wa'lŏ'kdi (above the last mentioned on the opposite side of the creek), waḳ'a'k (south of the high ridge south of Odessa), gai'lŏks or gaila'lḳs (on the point south of Odessa, or more probably between Howard and Shoalwater Bays), stŏ'kmatc (at Eagle Point); to which should perhaps be added: e'o'ḳaḳ (on Wood River, toward the mountains), and e'uḳwa'lksi (on the east side of Wood River, and possibly the same site as the other).

V. iu'la'loŋkni (the people of Klamath Falls (Link River) and the eastern shore of Klamath Lake), including the following villages: kᴇt!ai'ksi (extending southward from a promontory 2 miles or so northwest of Modoc Point), suwiakă'ĕks (at Modoc Point), iulă'u (on the east side of Klamath Lake), diu'wiaks (at the railroad point Ouxy), ḳau'ŏmŏt (a half mile south of the preceding on the lake shore), dĭ'tk!aḳs (at a hot spring known as Barclay Spring near the last mentioned), kŏlwa'l (at Rattlesnake Point at Algoma), wuḳ!o'twas (on Buck Island in Klamath Lake), lama'tcksi (on the point east of Buck Island), k!su'nk!si (three-fourths of a mile south of the preceding on the shore of Klamath Lake), iwau'wŏne (on both sides of Link River at the highway bridge), iu''laloŋe (at the mouth of Klamath River), wĕḳă'ĕls (on the shore of Klamath Lake a mile west of the mouth of Klamath River), wut!ana'kŏḳs (at one end of a little marsh (now drained) on the west side of Klamath Lake), iup!a'tŏna (at the other end of the same marsh), woksa'lks (on the north shore of Wokas marsh near Klamath Lake), dĕ'ktcŏŋks (on the west shore of Klamath Lake opposite Buck Island), sa'stĭtḳa'-wals (at Squaw Point).

Population.—Mooney (1928) estimated the Klamath at 800 in 1780 but Spier (1930) raises this to 1,200. In 1905, including former slaves and members of other tribes more or less assimilated with them, they numbered 755. The census of 1910 returned 696. In 1923 there were 1,201 Indians under the Klamath Superintendency including Klamath, Modoc, and other Indians. In 1930, 2,034 were returned as Klamath and Modoc. In 1937 the United States Office of Indian Affairs reported 1,912 Klamath.

Connection in which they have become noted.—The name Klamath is perpetuated by Klamath Lake, Klamath County, and the town of Klamath Falls, Klamath County, Oreg.; by Klamath River, Oreg. and Calif.; and by a village in Humboldt County, Calif.

Kuitsh. Significance unknown. Also called:

Ci-sta'-qwût-mê' tunnĕ', Mishikwutmetunne name, meaning "people dwelling on the stream called Shista."
Lower Umpqua, or Umpwua, popular name.
Tu'kwil-mă'-k'i, Alsea name.

Connections.—The Kuitsh belonged to the Yakonan linguistic stock, though so remotely connected that Frachtenberg (1911, p. 441) thought of placing them in an independent family, the Siuslawan.

Location.—On Lower Umpqua River.

Villages

According to Dorsey these were:

Chitlatamus.
Chukhuiyathl.
Chukukh.
Chupichnushkuch.
Kaiyuwuntsunitthai.
Khuwaihus.
Kthae.
Kuiltsh.
Mikulitsh.
Misun.
Ntsiyamis.
Paiuiyunitthai.
Skakhaus.
Takhaiya.
Thukhita.
Tkimeye.
Tsalila.
Tsetthim.
Tsiakhaus.
Tsunakthiamittha.
Wuituthlaa.

Population.—The Kuitsh are usually classed with the Siuslaw. Mooney (1928) estimates the entire Yakonan stock at 6,000 in 1780, and by 1930 this had been reduced to 9. The Kuitsh are nowhere separately enumerated.

Latgawa. Signifying "those living in the uplands." Also called:

Walumskni, by the Klamath.

Connections.—With the Takelma proper, the Latgawa constituted the Takilman linguistic family which, in turn, was probably affiliated with the Shastan stock.

Location.—On Upper Rogue River eastward about Table Rock and Bear Creek and in the neighborhood of the present town of Jacksonville.

Village

Sapir (1915) records one village belonging to this tribe known by the tribal name and also called Latgauk.

Population.—See **Takelma.**

Lohim. Significance unknown. (See **Paiute, Northern.**)

Connections.—Reported as a band of Shoshoneans which entered Oregon at a late period.

Location.—On Willow Creek, a southern affluent of the Columbia.

Population.—In 1870 the number of Lohim was reported as 114, but the name has not appeared in recent official reports. They have generally been regarded as renegades belonging to the Umatilla Reservation, and Ray's (1938) informants denied the presence of Shoshoneans here, asserting that the name was applied to Yakima.

Luckiamute, Lakmiut. Significance unknown.

> Alakĕma'yuk, Atfalati name.
> Suck-a-mier, Chelukimaukes, forms appearing in Reports of the Office of Indian Affairs.

Connections.—The Luckiamute belonged to the Calapooya dialectic division of the Kalapooian linguistic stock.

Location.—The Luckiamute River.

Subdivisions or Bands

Ampalamuyu, on Luckiamute River.
Mohawk, on Mohawk River.
Tsalakmiut, on Luckiamute River.
Tsamiak, near Luckiamute River.
Tsantatawa, south of Luckiamute River.
Tsantuisha, on Luckiamute River.

Population.—(See **Calapooya.**) The number of Luckiamute was given as 28 in 1905. The census of 1910 returned only 8.

Connection in which they have become noted.—This tribe has given its name to Luckiamute River, Oreg.

Miluk. Significance unknown; also called Lower Coquille.

Connections.—The Miluk spoke the southern of the two dialects of the Kusan linguistic family, and were related more remotely to the Yakonan stock.

Location.—At the mouth of Coquille River.

Villages

Miluk or Mulluk, on the north side of the Coquille River at the site of the present town of Randolph.
Nasumi, on the south side of Coquille River on the coast of Oregon, near the site of the present Bandon.

Population.—Mooney (1928) estimated 2,000 in 1780 for the Miluk and Hanis together. In 1910 they numbered 93. (See **Hanis.**) In 1937 the population of the "Kus" Indians was given as 55.

Mishikhwutmetunne. Signifying "people who live on the stream called Mishi." Also called:

> Coquille, or Upper Coquille, from their habitat.
> De-d'á tené, Tutuni name, meaning "people by the northern water."
> Ithalé tĕni, Umpqua name.
> Kukwil', Alsea name (from Coquille).

Connections.—The Mishikhwutmetunne belonged to the Athapascan linguistic stock, their relations being particularly close with the Tututni.

Location.—On upper Coquille River.

Villages

The following were recorded by J. O. Dorsey (1884):

Chockreletan, near the forks of Coquille River.
Chuntshataatunne.
Duldulthawaiame.
Enitunne.
Ilsethlthawaiame.
Katomemetunne.
Khinukhtunne.
Khweshtunne, next above Coquille City.
Kimestunne.
Kthukhwestunne.
Kthunataachuntunne.
Meshtshe.
Nakhituntunne
Nakhochatunne.
Natarghiliitunne.
Natsushltatunne.
Nilestunne.
Rghoyinestunne.
Sathlrekhtun.
Sekhushtuntunne.
Sunsunnestunne.
Sushltakhotthatunne.
Thlkwantiyatunne.
Thltsharghiliitunne.
Thltsusmetunne.
Thlulchikhwutmetunne.
Timethltunne.
Tkhlunkhastunne, next to the Kusan people and below Coquille City.
Tsatarghekhetunne
Tthinatlitunne, at the site of Coquille.
Tulwutmetunne.
Tuskhlustunne.
Tustatunkhuushi.

Drucker (1937) recorded besides:

Hweshtun (perhaps partly Kusan).
Natgrilitun.
Stonerutltutl, a suburb of Natgrilitun.
Tlunhoshtun, said to have come from Umpqua.

Population.—(See **Chastacosta.**) The census of 1910 returned 15 Mishikhwutmetunne under the name Upper Coquille.

Modoc. From Móatokni, meaning "southerners." Also called:

Aígspaluma, Nez Percé name for all Indians on Klamath Reservation and in the vicinity.
La-la-cas, said to be the original name.
Lutmáwi, by a part of the Pit River Indians.
Lutuami, Ilmawi name.
Pχánai, Yreka Shasta name.
Saidoka, Shoshoni name.

Connections.—With the Klamath (q. v.), the Modoc constituted the Lutuamian division of the Shapwailutan linguistic stock.

Location.—On Little Klamath Lake, Modoc Lake, Tule Lake, Lost River Valley, and Clear Lake, extending at times as far east as Goose Lake. (See also California and Oklahoma.)

Subdivisions

The most important bands of the Modoc are said to have been at Little Klamath Lake, Tule Lake, and in the valley of Lost River.

Villages

Agawesh, on lower Klamath Lake, Calif., and on Hot Creek.
Chakawech, near Yaneks, on Sprague River, Klamath Reservation.
Kalelk, on the north shore of Tule or Rhett Lake.

Kawa, at Yaneks on Sprague River.
Keshlakchuis, on the southeast side of Tule (Rhett) Lake, Calif.
Keuchishkeni, on Hot Creek near Little Klamath Lake, Calif.
Kumbatuash (with Klamath), southwest of Tule (Rhett) Lake, Calif., extending from the lake shore to the lava beds.
Leush, on the north side of Tule (Rhett) Lake, Oreg.
Nakoshkeni, at the junction of Lost River with Tule Lake.
Nushaltkagakni, at the headwaters of Lost River near Bonanna.
Pashka, on the northwest shore of Tule (Rhett) Lake.
Shapashkeni, on the southeast side of Little Klamath Lake, Calif.
Sputuishkeni, on Lower Klamath Lake, Calif.
Stuikishkeni, on the north side of Little Klamath Lake.
Waisha, on Lost River, 3 or 4 miles northwest of Tule Lake, and near the hills that culminate in Laki Peak.
Wachamshwash, on Lost River near Tule (Rhett) Lake, in Klamath County.
Welwashkeni, on the southeast side of Tule Lake, at Miller's Farm, Calif.
Wukakeni, on the east side of Tule Lake, Calif.
Yaneks (with Klamath and Shoshoni), along middle Sprague River, Lake County.
Yulalona (with Klamath), at the site of the present Linkville.

History.—The Modoc came into contact with the Whites in comparatively late times, and acquired an unfortunate reputation from frequent conflicts with white immigrants in which atrocities were committed on both sides. In 1864 the Modoc and the Klamath together ceded their territory to the United States and retired to Klamath Reservation, but they were never contented there and made persistent efforts to return to their old country. Finally, in 1870, a chief named Kintpuash, better known to the Whites as Captain Jack, led the more turbulent element of the tribe back to the California border and refused to return. The first attempt to bring the runaways back precipitated the Modoc War of 1872–73. The Modoc retreated to the lava beds of northern California and for several months resisted all attempts to dislodge them, but they were finally overcome and Kintpuash and five other leaders hanged in October of that year. Part of the tribe was then sent to Indian Territory and placed on the Quapaw Reservation and the remainder on the Klamath Reservation.

Population.—Mooney (1928) estimates that there were 400 Modoc in 1780, but Kroeber (1925), with whom Spier (1930) seems to concur, allows twice as many. In 1905 there were 56 on the Quapaw Reservation and 223 on the Klamath Reservation. The census of 1910 returned 282, of whom 212 were in Oregon, 33 in Oklahoma, 20 in California, and the remainder scattered among 5 other States. In 1930 31 were in Oklahoma. (See **Klamath.**) In 1937, 329 were reported.

Connections in which they have become noted.—The chief claim of the Modoc to remembrance is on account of the remarkable defensive war they maintained in the lava beds of California, as above stated. A California county is named for them and places called Modoc are to be found in Phillips County, Ark.; in Emanuel County, Ga.; in Louisiana; in Ohio; and in McCormick County, S. C.; Randolph County, Ill.; and Randolph County, Ind.; also in the name of Modoc Point, Oreg.; in Scott County, Kans.; and in the name of the Modoc Lava Beds, Calif.

Molala. Derived from the name of a creek in the Willamette Valley from which one of their bands drove the original inhabitants. Also called:

Amolélish, by the Kalapuya.
Kúikni, by the Klamath.
Láti-u or La'tiwĕ, their own name.
Ya'-ide'sta, by the Umpqua.

Connections.—Together with the Cayuse, the Molala constituted the Waiilatpuan division of the Shapwailutan linguistic stock. According to Cayuse tradition, the Molala formerly lived with them and were separated and driven westward in consequence of wars with hostile tribes.

Location.—At an early date the Molala are believed to have been in the valley of the Deschutes River and to have been driven west, as above intimated, into the valleys of the Molala and Santiam Rivers. Either part of them subsequently went south to the headwaters of Umpqua and Rogue Rivers or they were separated from the rest in the movement above mentioned, as Berreman (1937) thinks.

Subdivisions

The following are said to have been Molala bands or settlements:

Chakankni, on the headwaters of Rogue River, northwest of Klamath Lake, absorbed later by the neighboring tribes, particularly the Klamath.
Chimbuiha, on the headwaters of Santiam River.
Mukanti, on the western slope of the Cascade Mountains.

Population.—Mooney (1928) believes the Molala were still with the Cayuse in 1780, whose numbers he fixes at about 500. In 1849 the Molala were estimated at 100. In 1877 Gatschet found several families living on the Grande Ronde Reservation, and in 1881 there were said to be 20 individuals in the mountains west of Klamath Lake. The census of 1910 returned 31, all but 6 of whom were in Oregon. (See **Cayuse.**)

Connection in which they have become noted.—The Molala are noteworthy in the first place for the uniqueness of their language, which is closely related only to Cayuse. Molalla River or Creek and a post village, both in Clackamas County, Oreg., bear the name.

Multnomah. Significance unknown. Also called:

Wappato, originally the Cree or Chippewa name of a bulbous root (*Sagittaria variabilis*) used as food by the Indians of the west and northwest It means literally "white fungus." It passed into the Chinook jargon with the meaning "potato" and became applied to Sauvies Island in Columbia River, at the mouth of the Willamette, and the Indian tribes living on or near it. It was so used by Lewis and Clark, though there was little or no political connection between the numerous bands so designated.

Connections.—The Multnomah belonged to the Clackamas division of the Chinookan linguistic stock.

Location.—As above indicated, on and near Sauvies Island.

Subdivisions or Bands

Cathlacomatup, on the south side of Sauvies Island on a slough of Willamette River.

Cathlacumup on the west bank of the lower mouth of the Willamette River and claiming as their territory the bank of the Columbia from there to Deer Island.

Cathlanaquiah, on the southwest side of Sauvies Island.

Clahnaquah, on Sauvies Island.

Claninnata, on the southwest side of Sauvies Island.

Kathlaminimin, at the south end of Sauvies Island, later said to have become associated with the Cathlacumup and Nemoit.

Multnomah, on the upper end of Sauvies Island.

Nechacokee, on the south bank of Columbia River a few miles below Quicksand (Sandy) River.

Nemalquinner, at the falls of the Willamette but with a temporary house on the north end of Sauvies Island.

Shoto, on the north side of Columbia River, a short distance from it and nearly opposite the mouth of the Willamette.

Population.—Mooney (1928) gives the population of all of these bands of the Multnomah as 3,600 in 1780. Their descendants are probably included among the 315 Indians returned as Chinook by the census of 1910. (See **Clackamas.**)

Connection in which they have become noted.—There is a county, town, and river channel of the name in Oregon. The name "Wappato" secondarily applied to the Multnomah besides its former use as a name of Sauvies Island, is given, with the spelling Sapato, to a lake and place near Portland in Oregon—the latter in Multnomah County, the former between Yamhill and Washington Counties—and to a place in the State of Washington.

Naltunnetunne, a small Athapascan tribe between the Tututni and Chetco, apparently included by later writers under the former.

Nez Percé. They extended into northeastern Oregon. (See Idaho.)

Paiute, Northern. These people occupied the southeastern part of Oregon and formerly extended far enough north to include the valley of Powder River and the upper course of John Day River of which they were dispossessed by Shahaptians. (See Nevada.)

Santiam. Significance unknown. Also called:

Aha'lpam, by the Atfalati Kalapuya.

Connections.—The Santiam belonged to the Calapooya dialectic division of the Kalapooian linguistic stock.

Location.—Santiam River.

Subdivisions or Bands

Chamifu, on Yamhill Creek.
Chanchampenau, east of Willamette River.
Chanchantu, location not specified.
Chantkaip, below the junction of the Santiam forks.

Population.—(See **Calapooya**.) In 1906 there were 23 Santiam on Grande Ronde Reservation. The census of 1910 returned 9.

Connection in which they have become noted.—The name Santiam is perpetuated in Santiam River, a branch of the Willamette.

Shasta. The Shasta extended at least into the territory watered by Jenny Creek from their main seats in California (q. v.).

Siletz. Significance unknown. Also called:

Tsä Shnádsh amím, Luckiamute Kalapuya name.

Connections.—The Siletz belonged to the Salishan linguistic stock.

Location.—On Siletz River.

Population.—Mooney (1928) estimates the population of all of the Salishan tribes of Oregon as 1,500 in 1780. They are not now separately recorded, but in the census of 1930, 72 Salishan Indians were returned from Oregon besides the Tillamook.

Connections in which they have become noted.—The Siletz are of note as having been the southernmost of the Salishan linguistic family. Siletz River and a post village, both in Lincoln County, Oreg., preserve the name.

Siuslaw. Significance unknown. Also called:

K'çu-qwĭc'tûnnĕ, Naltunne name.
K'qlo-qwec tûnnĕ, Chastacosta name.
Tsaná-uta amím, Luckiamute Kalapuya name.

Connections.—The Siuslaw belonged to the Siuslawan division of the Yakonan linguistic stock.

Location.—On and near Siuslaw River.

Villages

Dorsey (1884) gives the following:

Chimuksaich.
Hauwiyat.
Hilakwitiyus.
Khachtais.
Khaikuchum.
Khaiyumitu.
Khakhaich.
Khalakw.
Kumiyus.
Kumkwu.
Kupimithlta.
Kuskussu.
Kwsichichu (south of Eugene City).
Kwulhauunnich.

Kwultsaiya.
Kwunnumis.
Kwuskwemus.
Matsnikth.
Mithlausmintthai.
Paauwis.
Pia.
Pilumas.
Pithlkwutsiaus.
Skhutch.
Stthukhwich.
Thlachaus.
Thlekuaus.
Tiekwachi.
Tsahais.
Tsatauwis.
Tsiekhaweyathl.
Waitus.
Wetsiaus.
Yukhwustitu.

Population.—(See **Alsea**.) The census of 1910 reported 7 Siuslaw.

Connection in which they have become noted.—The name Siuslaw is preserved by Siuslaw River, in Lane County, Oreg.

Skilloot. The Skilloot occupied part of Oregon opposite the mouth of Cowlitz River. (See Washington.)

Snake. (See **Northern Paiute** under Nevada.)

Takelma. Own name, meaning "those dwelling along the river."

Kyu'-kŭtc hĭtclŭm, Alsea name meaning "people far down the stream (or country)."
Lowland Takelma, of Berreman (1937).
Na-tcté tûnnĕ, Naltunne name.
Rogue River Indians, from their habitat.

Connections.—Together with the Latgawa (q. v.), the Takelma constituted the Takilman linguistic stock. It is possible that this is distantly connected with the Shastan stock of northern California.

Location.—On the middle course of Rogue River from above Illinois River to about Grant's Pass and on the northern tributaries of Rogue River between these limits and the upper course of Cow Creek; also south nearly to the California boundary.

Villages

The following names were recorded by J. O. Dorsey mainly in one of the Athapascan dialects of the region:

Hashkushtun, on the south side of Rogue River.
Hudedut, at the forks of Rogue River and Applegate River.
Kashtata, on the south side of Rogue River above Leaf Creek and Galice Creek.
Kthotaime, on the south side of Rogue River.
Nakila, on the south side of Rogue River about 10 miles above Yaasitun.
Salwahka, near the mouth of Illinois River or one of its tributaries.
Seethltun, on the south side of Rogue River, the village nearest the Chastacosta.
Sestikustun, on the south side of Rogue River.
Sewaathlchutun, ibid.
Shkashtun, ibid.
Skanowethltunne, ibid.
Talmamiche, ibid.
Talotunne, ibid.

Tthowache, on the south side of Rogue River near "Deep Rock".
Yaasitun, on the south side of Rogue River.
Yushlali, ibid.

The following names, probably covering in part the same towns, were recorded by Dr. Edward Sapir in 1906, and are enumerated from the Latgawa country downstream:

Hatil, east of Table Rock.
Gelyalk, below Table Rock.
Dilomi, near the falls of Rogue River.
Gwenpunk.
Hayaalbalsda.
Daktgamik.
Didalam, on the present site of Grant's Pass, the county seat of Josephine County.
Daktsasin or Daldanik, on Rogue River near Jump Off Joe Creek.
Hagwal, on Cow Creek.
Somouluk.
Hatonk.

Population.—Mooney (1928) estimates the entire Takilman stock at 500 in 1780. Only 1 was returned under that name by the census of 1910, but under the general head of "Rogue River" the Indian Office Report for 1937 gives two bodies of Indians numbering 58 and 46 individuals, respectively.

Connection in which they have become noted.—Together with the Latgawa, the Takelma are remarkable for the peculiarity of their language, accentuated by the fact that they are almost entirely surrounded by Athapascan peoples. A post village called Takilma in Josephine County, Oreg., perpetuates the name.

Taltushtuntude. Own name, meaning unknown. Also called:

> Galice Creek Indians, from their habitat.
> Kû-lĭs'-kitc hĭtc'lûm, Alsea name.

Connections.—The Taltushtuntude belonged to the Athapascan linguistic stock, and spoke the same dialect as the Dakubetede but culturally had become assimilated with the Takelma.

Location.—On Galice Creek.

Population.—In 1856, 18 Taltushtuntude were reported living on the Siletz Reservation. Under the name "Galice Creek" 42 Indians were reported in 1937.

Tenino. Significance unknown. Also called:

> Mĕli'-lĕma, own name.
> Warm Springs Indians, the common official designation.

Connections.—The Tenino constituted a division of the Shahaptian branch of the Shapwailutan linguistic stock.

Subdivisions and Villages

Kowasayee, on the north bank of Columbia River nearly opposite the mouth of the Umatilla.

Ochechote or Uchichol, on the north bank of Columbia River, the exact region being uncertain though they derive their name from a rock near the mouth of the Deschutes River.

Skinpah, on the north bank of Columbia River above the mouth of the Deschutes.

Tapanash, on the north bank of Columbia River, near the mouth of the Deschutes and a little above Celilo, the name being later extended over most of the above bands.

Tilkuni, between White and Warm Springs Reservations.

Tukspush on John Day River, and hence called often John Day Indians.

Wahopum, on the north bank of Columbia River near the mouth of Olive Creek.

Waiam, near the mouth of the Deschutes River.

History.—The Tenino were mentioned by Lewis and Clark in 1805. By the treaty of 1855 they gave up their lands and settled, along with other Shahaptian tribes and some Salishan tribes, on Yakima Reservation, Washington. Since then they have not had separate official recognition.

Population.—Mooney (1928) estimated that in 1780 there were 3,600 including the Atanum of the Yakima and the Tyigh. The United States Office of Indian Affairs reported 460 in 1937 of the Yakima and associated bands.

Connection in which they have become noted.—A town in Thurston County, Wash., perpetuates the name.

Tillamook. A Chinook term meaning "people of Nekelim (or Nehalem). Also spelled Calamox, Gillamooks, Killamook, etc.

Higgahaldahu, Nestucca name.

Kyaukw, Alsea name.

Nsietshawas, so called by Hale (1846).

Si ni'-tĕ-lĭ, Mishikwutmetunne name for this tribe and the Alsea, meaning "flatheads."

Connections.—The Tillamook were the principal tribe in Oregon belonging to the Salishan linguistic family, coastal division.

Location.—The coast from the Nehalem to Salmon River.

Subdivisions and Villages

Nehalem, on Nehalem River.

Nestucca, on Nestucca Bay and the streams flowing into it.

Salmon River, on the river of that name.

Tillamook, on Tillamook Bay and the streams flowing into it, including the following villages enumerated by Lewis and Clark: Chishucks (at the mouth of Tillamook River), Chucktin (the southernmost Tillamook village, on a creek emptying into Tillamook Bay), Kilherhursh (at the entrance of Tillamook Bay), Kilherner (on Tillamook Bay, at the mouth of a creek 2 miles from Kilherhursh), Towerquotten (on a creek emptying into Tillamook Bay).

Population.—See **Siletz**. Lewis and Clark estimated 2,200 Tillamook in 1805. In the reports of the Wilkes Exploring Expedition (1845) their number is given as 400, and by Lane in 1849 as 200. The census of 1910 returned 25, and that of 1930, 12.

Connection in which they have become noted.—The Tillamook seem to have been the most powerful tribe on the coast of Oregon. A bay, and also a county and its capital in the former country of the tribe preserve the name; also a cape, Tillamook Head.

Tututni. Meaning unknown. Also called:

H'lilush, Nestucca name.
Lower Rogue River Indians, or Rogue River Indians, from their habitat.
Tálĕmaya, Umpqua name.
Ta-qu'-qûc-cĕ, Chetco name, meaning "northern language."

Connections.—The Tututni belonged to the Athapascan linguistic stock, and were related closely with the Mishikhwutmetunne.

Location.—On lower Rogue River and the Pacific coast north and south of its mouth.

Villages

J. O. Dorsey (1884) gave the following villages or bands:

On the north coast of Rogue River:
Chemetunne, popularly called Joshuas, just north of Rogue River.
Kaltsergheatunne, at Port Orford.
Kosotshe, between Port Orford and Sixes Creek, perhaps earlier on Flores Creek.
Kwatami, on or near Sixes River.
Kthukwuttunne.
Kthutetmeseetuttun, just north of Rogue River.
Kwusathlkhuntunne, said to have been at the mouth of Mussel Creek, 5 miles south of Mount Humbug.
Natutshltunne, between Coquille River and Flores Creek.
Niletunne, the first village south of the Miluk village of Nasumi, south of Coquille River.
Yukichetunne, on Euchre Creek.

On Rogue River:
Chetlesiyetunne, on the north side.
Enitunne, near the mouth of a southern affluent of Rogue River.
Etaatthetunne.
Kunechuta.
Kushetunne, on the north side.
Mikonotunne, on the north side 14 miles from its mouth.
Nakatkhaitunne, on the north side of Rogue River.
Targheliichetunne, on the north side.
Targhutthotunne, near the coast.
Testthitun, on the north side.
Thechuntunne, on the north side.
Thethlkhttunne, or Chastacosta, on the north side.

On or near the coast south of Rogue River:

Chetleschantunne, on Pistol River and the headlands from the coast 6 miles south of Rogue River.
Khainanaitetunne.
Kheerghia, about 25 miles south of Pistol River.
Khwaishtunnetunne, near the mouth of a small stream locally called Wishtenatin, after the name of the settlement, that enters the Pacific about 10 miles south of Pistol River, at a place later known as Hustenate.
Natthutunne, on the south side of Rogue River.
Nuchumatuntunne, on the north side of Rogue River near the mouth.
Sentethltun, on the south side of Rogue River and perhaps at its mouth.
Skumeme, on the south side of Rogue River near its mouth.
Tsetintunne, the highest of 4 villages on a stream emptying into Rogue River near its mouth.
Tsetuttunne.

Drucker (1937) gives the following village names:

On Rogue River:

Gwī'sat huntun, on Mussel Creek near Sixes River and sometimes separated as the Sixes tribe.
Kusū'me, on what is now called Flores Creek.
Kwataime, a short distance north of last.
Kwuse'tun, near and possibly a suburb of Megwinō'tun, on the coast.
Megwinō'tun, a few miles up river.
Skame'me, between Pistol River and mouth of Rogue River; Waterman places it at Hunter's Creek.
Sukwe'me or Sukwe'tce, at mouth of Sixes River.
Tagrilī'tun, a suburb of Tū'tutun.
Tce'metun or Tce'me, really two towns, one on each side of the river's mouth.
Tce'tlersh tcuntun, on Pistol River, perhaps belonging to the Chetco.
Tū'tutun, 5 to 6 miles from the river's mouth, divided into two parts called Tatre'tun, "downriver," and Na'gutretun "upriver."
Yukwī'tce or Yu'gwitce, on what is now called Euchre Creek.

Berreman (1937) makes seven major divisions as follows: Kwatami or Sixes River; Euchre Creek (Yukichetunne); Mikono tunne; Pistol River (Chetleschantunne); Joshua; Tututunne (Tututni); Kwaishtunne or Khustenete.

Population.—(See **Chastacosta.**) In 1854 the Tututni population was 1,311. The census of 1910 returned 383, but in 1930 the United States Indian Office gave only 41 under this name, 55 under that of "Meguenodon" (see above), and 45 under that of "Joshua" (Tce'metun).

Tyigh. Significance unknown. Also spelled Attayes, Iyich, Ta-ih, Thy, Tyh, etc.

Teáχtkni, or Télknikni, Klamath name.
Tsĕ Amínĕma, Luckiamute Kalapuya name.

Connections.—The Tyigh belonged to the Tenino branch of the Shahaptian division of the Shapwailutan linguistic stock.

Location.—The country about Tygh and White Rivers.

Subdivisions and Villages

No names are recorded.

History.—The history of the Tyigh was identical with that of the Tenino (q. v.).

Population.—With the other Oregon tribes of the Tenino group, the Tyigh numbered 1,400 in 1780 according to Mooney's (1928) estimate. In 1854 they were said to number 500 and in 1859, 450; but both of these figures must be overestimates. They are not now enumerated separately from the Warm Spring Indians, placed at 550 by the census of 1910.

Connection in which they have become noted.—Tygh Creek and a place called Tygh Valley in Wasco County, Oreg., bears the name of the Tyigh.

Umatilla. Significance unknown.

Connections.—The Umatilla belonged to the Shahaptian division of the Shapwailutan linguistic stock.

Location.—On Umatilla River and the banks of Columbia River adjacent to the mouth of the Umatilla.

Population.—Mooney (1928) estimates this tribe and the Wallawalla together at 1,500 in 1780. The census of 1910 returned 272, the United States Indian Office Report for 1923, 145, and the Indian Office Report for 1937, 124.

Connections in which they have become noted.—An Indian reservation has received the name Umatilla, and it has also been applied to a river, a county, and a post village, all in Oregon; also to a place in Lake County, Fla.

Umpqua. Significance unknown.

Amgútsuish, Shasta name.
Cactaⁿ'-qwût-me'tûnnĕ, Naltunne name.
Ci-cta'-qwŭt-me'tûnnĕ, Tututni name, meaning "Umpqua River people."
Ci-sta'-qwût, Chastacosta name.
Etnémitane, own name (Gatschet, 1877).
Tsan Ámpkua amím, Luckiamute Kalapuya name, meaning "people on the Umpqua."
Upper Umpqua, Berreman (1937).
Yaᵃgalá', Takelma name.

Connections.—The Umpqua belonged to the Athapascan linguistic stock.

Location.—On upper Umpqua River, east of the Kuitsh.

Subdivisions

The Umpqua on Cow Creek are often spoken of separately under the name Nahankhuotana. Parker (1840) mentions a people called Palakahu which was probably an Athapascan or Yakonan tribe but cannot now be identified, and also the Skoton and Chasta, probably parts of the Chastacosta or Tututni. This is all the more likely as he includes the Kwatami band of the Tututni and the entirely independent Chilula of California. Their chief village was Hewut.

Population.—(See **Dakubetede.**) Hale (1846) says that in his time the Umpqua were supposed to number not more than 400. In 1902 there were 84 on Grande Ronde Reservation. The census of 1910 returned 109. In 1937, 43 Indians are given under this name. (See **Chastacosta** and **Dakubetede.**)

Connection in which they have become noted.—Umpqua River, and the settlement of Umpqua or Umpqua Ferry in Douglas County, preserve the name.

Wallawalla. The Wallawalla extended somewhat into northeastern Oregon. (See Washington.)

Walpapi. Significance unknown. Commonly called Snakes. A part of the Northern Paiute. (See under Nevada.)

Wasco. From a native word wacq!ó, "cup or small bowl of horn," the reference being to a cup-shaped rock a short distance from the main village of the tribe; from this the tribal name Gałasq'ó, "those that have the cup," is derived and variations of it frequently appear in the literature. Also called:

Afúlakin, by the Kalapuya.
Ámpxänkni, meaning "where the water is," by the Klamath.
Awásko ammim, by the Kalapuya.
Sáxlatks, by the Molala.

Connections.—They belonged to the upstream branch of the Chinookan linguistic stock, their closest relatives being the Wishram on the opposite side of the river.

Location.—In the neighborhood of The Dalles, in the present Wasco County.

Villages and Fishing Stations

The following are given by Sapir (1930) in order from east to west: Hlgahacha, Igiskhis, Wasco (a few miles above the present town of The Dalles), Wogupan, Natlalalaik, Gawobumat, Hliekala-imadik, Wikatk, Watsokus, Winkwot (at The Dalles), Hlilwaihldik, Hliapkenum, Kabala, Gayahisitik, Itkumahlemkt, Hlgaktahlk, Tgahu, Hliluktik, Gahlentlich, Gechgechak, Skhlalis.

Population.—Morse (1822) estimated the number of Wasco at 900. The census of 1910 returned 242, and the United States Office of Indian Affairs, 227 in 1937. (See **Clackamas** and **Watlala.**)

Connections in which they have become noted.—The Wasco were the strongest Upper Chinook tribe and that which ultimately absorbed the rest. The name is preserved by Wasco County, Oreg., and a town in Sherman County in the same State; also places in Kern County, Calif., and Kane County, Ill.

877646—52——31

Watlala. Significance of word is unknown. Also called:

Cascade Indians, the popular English name.
Gila'xicatck, by the Chinook.
Katlagakya, own name.
Shahala, from Chinook saxala, meaning "above," by Chinook.

Connections.—The Watlala belonged to the Chinookan linguistic stock and the Clackamas dialectic group.

Location.—At the Cascades of Columbia River and extending down to the mouth of the Willamette River.

Subdivisions

The following names have been applied by various writers to the Indians in this neighborhood and may be subdivisions of this tribe, or perhaps refer to the entire tribe itself:

Cathlakaheckit, at the Cascades.
Cathlathlala, just below the Cascades.
Clahclellah, near the foot of the Cascades.
Neerchokioon, on the south side of Columbia River a few miles above Sauvies Island.
Washougal, near Quicksand River.
Yehuh, just above the Cascades.

Population.—Mooney (1928) estimates that the Watlala and the Wasco together numbered 3,200 in 1780. In 1805–6 Lewis and Clark estimated that there were 2,800. In 1812 the two first-mentioned bands were estimated to number 1,400. They are no longer enumerated separately and are probably incorporated at the present time with the Wishram and the Wasco.

Yahuskin. One of the two chief peoples in Oregon belonging to the Northern Paiute division of the Shoshonean and therefore Uto-Aztecan linguistic stock. (See Nevada.)

Yamel. Significance unknown, often spelled Yam Hill. Also called:

Ychă-yamel-amim, by the Atfalati Kalapuya.

Connections.—The Yamel belonged, along with the Atfalati, to the northern dialectic division of the Kalapooian linguistic stock.

Location.—Yamhill River.

Subdivisions

Gatschet (1877) records these as follows:

Andshankualth, on a western tributary of the Willamette.
Andshimmampak, on Yamhill River.
Chamifu, in the forks of Yamhill River.
Chamiwi, on Yamhill River.
Champikle, on Dallas (La Creole) Creek.
Chinchal, on Dallas Creek.

Population.—(See **Calapooya.**) The census of 1910 returned 5 Yamel.

Connection in which they have become noted.—The name of the Yamel, in the form Yamhill, is perpetuated by an affluent of the Willamette and by the county through which it flows.

Yaquina. Significance unknown.

Să-ákl, Nestucca name.
Sĭs′-qûn-me′tûnnĕ, Chetco name.
Tcha yákon amim, Luckiamute Kalapuya name.

Connections.—The Yaquina were one of the tribes of the Yakonan linguistic stock to which they gave their name.

Location.—About Yaquina River and Bay.

Villages

The following list is from J. O. Dorsey (1884):

On the north side of Yaquina River:

Holukhik.
Hunkkhwitik.
Iwai.
Khaishuk.
Khilukh.
Kunnupiyu.
Kwulaishauik.
Kyaukuhu.
Kyuwatkal.
Mipshuntik.
Mittsulstik.
Shash.
Thlalkhaiuntik.
Thlekakhaik.
Tkhakiyu.
Tshkitshiauk.
Tthilkitik.
Ukhwaiksh.
Yahal.
Yikkhaich.

On the south side of the river:

Atshuk.
Chulithltiyu.
Hakkyaiwal.
Hathletukhish.
Hitshinsuwit.
Hiwaitthe.
Kaku.
Khaiyukkhai.
Khitalaitthe.
Kholkh.
Khulhanshtauk.
Kilauutuksh.
Kumsukwum.
Kutshuwitthe.
Kwaitshi.
Kwilaishauk.
Kwulchichicheshk.
Kwullaish.
Kwullakhtauik.
Kwutichuntthe.
Mulshintik.
Naaish.
Paiinkhwutthu.
Pikiiltthe.
Pkhulluwaaitthe.
Pkuuniukhtauk.
Puuntthiwaun.
Shilkhotshi.
Shupauk.
Thlekwiyauik.
Thlelkhus.
Thlinaitshtik.
Thlukwiutshthu.
Tkulmashaauk.
Tuhaushuwitthe.
Tulshk.

Population.—(See **Alsea.**) The census of 1910 returned 19 Yaquina.

Connecton in which they have become noted.—The name of this tribe Yaquina, was given some scientific prominence by its use, in the form

Yakonan, for a small linguistic stock in the Powellian classification. It is preserved in Yaquina River, Yaquina Bay and a town called Yaquina in Lincoln County.

Yoncalla. From Ayankēld, or Tch'Ayankē'ld, "those living at Ayankeld," own name.

Connections.—The Yoncalla were the southernmost tribe of the Kalapooian linguistic stock, forming one of the three dialectic divisions.

Location.—On Elk and Calapooya Creeks, tributaries of Umpqua River.

Subdivisions

According to Gatschet (1887), there were two bands, called Chayankeld and Tsantokayu by the Luckiamute, but it seems likely that the former name (Tch' Ayankē'ld) is merely the native tribal name.

Population.—(See **Calapooya.**) The census of 1910 returned 11 Yoncalla.

Connection in which they have become noted.—Yoncalla, a post village of Douglas County, Oreg., preserves the name.

INDIAN GIRLS AND CANOE, PUGET SOUND.

SOME NOTES

There are some minor and unimportant errors on page 16 of this booklet. Few historians today would find the story of the voyage of Juan de Fuca to the Northwest Coast of America to be much more acceptable than the apocryphal accounts of Fonte and Maldenado. Although the Hudson's Bay Company was chartered in 1670 and the Northwest Company was organized in the winter of 1783-1784 there was no representative of the Northwest Company in the inland Pacific Northwest before David Thompson built Kootanae House near Lake Windermere, now British Columbia, in 1807. He did not reach the mouth of the Columbia until the afternoon of July 15, 1811. The Hudson's Bay Company was not legally represented in the Pacific Northwest until the two companies merged in 1821 and for practical purposes not until Dr. John McLoughlin arrived in 1824. The first Christian missionaries were Indians. The first regular missions were Protestant, starting with the Willamette Mission of Jason Lee in 1834. Marcus Whitman and Henry Harman Spaulding did not arrive until 1836. There were no Catholic missionaries on the Coast before Fathers Blanchet and Demers in 1838. Pierre-Jean De Smet established St. Mary's in the Bitter Root valley in 1841, and Father Nicholas Point and Brother Huet founded the Sacred Heart Mission among the Coeur d'Alenes in 1842.

COLOPHON

The John Reed Swanton INDIAN TRIBES OF WASHINGTON, AND IDAHO, *was printed in the workshop of Glen Adams, which is located in the quiet country village of Fairfield, southern Spokane County in Washington state and one township removed from the Idaho line. Fairfield is located on state highway 27 that runs between Opportunity and Tekoa. Printing plates were made by Susan Paulson. The sheets were run by Vern Stevens using a 28 inch Heidelberg press model KORS. Folding was by Garry Adams using a three stage Baum Dial-O-Matic 16x40 folding machine. The hard case binding was done by Al Chidester, of Oakesdale, Washington Paper copies were bound by Glen Adams and Garry Adams. The paper stock is Island Offset, a Canadian sheet. This was a fun project. We had no special difficulty with the work*

CHINOOK WOMAN AND CHILD